LOU ANN SMITH

BE

DECISIVE!

MW01534799

"Good decisions open opportunities...move you closer to your goals...increase your potential. Good decisions attract dynamic people to your cause. Good decisions are a magnet for wealth."
— Stedman Graham
Author, *You Can Make It Happen*

"Learning and innovation are nothing without decision."
— Philip Crosby
Former Vice President, ITT
Author, *The Absolutes of Leadership*

"An important thing happens every time we make a decision — we come closer to knowing who we really are."
— Roger Dawson
Author, *The Confident Decision Maker*

"Top CEOs and executives know that intuition is what their best decisions are made of."
— Laura Berman Fortgang
Author, *Take Yourself to the Top*

"We must make decisions and learn to live with them. The quality that makes a great manager is decisiveness!"
— Lee Iacocca
Past President,
Chrysler Corporation

"Successful people not only have goals, they have goals that are meaningful for them. They know where they are going and they enjoy the trek."

– Marsha Sinetar, Ph.D.
Author, *Do What You Love,*
The Money Will Follow

"Presidents of corporations and countries are strong decision-makers. In a whirlwind of options, they have learned to selectively build bridges, or burn them, courageously and concisely choosing the future."

– Lou Ann Smith, quoted from
The Sacramento Bee Newspaper

How do they do it?

LOU ANN SMITH, in her practical and easy to read style will introduce you to six steps mastered by highly successful people. Follow the formula in this book and you, too, can BE DECISIVE!

Lou Ann Smith

BE
DECISIVE!

A Six Step Formula For Making Your Best Decisions
Every Time!

CYL BOOKS

Change Your Life Books
Mailing Address: P. O. Box 287
Rescue, California 95672

BE DECISIVE!
A Six Step Formula For Making Your Best Decisions
<u>Every Time</u>!

by Lou Ann Smith

CYL   Change Your Life Books
BOOKS   Mailing Address:
            P. O. Box 287
            Rescue, California 95672

Copyright © 1999 by Lou Ann Smith

Originally published in paperback in 1999 by
Change Your Life Books

All rights reserved, including the right to reproduce this
book or portions thereof in any form whatsoever.
For information address Change Your Life Books,
P. O. Box 287, Rescue, CA 95672

ISBN: 0-9669032-0-X

First Change Your Life Books trade paperback printing
January 1999

Cover design by Jim Weems of AD GRAPHICS
Cover Photograph by Kirby L. Smith
Text design by AD GRAPHICS, Tulsa, OK · 800-368-6196

Printed in the U.S.A.

Dedication

For Kirby

*So far we have
lived out 26 years
of our best-ever decision:
us*

Contents

Guess What?

Guess what?

Your decisions will not please everyone all the time. Get over it. Then get on with it. Allow me to emphasize this again. Be comforted and affirmed by it:

One hundred percent of the decisions you make will not please one hundred percent of the people you know one hundred percent of the time.

SO WHAT?

Be decisive anyway! The most important change you can make in your life this very minute is to become more decisive. I hope you picked up this book because you want to learn to act on information quickly and correctly.

You want to stop second guessing yourself. You want to make better use of your time. You want to live in balance, without regrets.

YOU CAN!

Here's how...

ONE

FOCUS

*There is no future
in a lack of vision.*

– Robert Miller,
Vice President of Marketing
Federal Express Corporation

————————

*You have to get the picture.
You have to see what you want
to achieve in your mind's eye.
Make it so you can smell it,
feel it, and see it in your mind
in 3-D Technicolor. It must be
so vivid you want to reach out
and grab it!*

– Roy Saunderson, Founder
Recognition Management Institute
London, Ontario, Canada

FOCUS

Imagine flying on a DC 10 commercial airplane. Suddenly your pilot's voice resonates over the public address system: "Ladies and gentlemen I would like to have your attention," he states and then clears his throat. "I have good news and bad news!

First the BAD news: UNFORTUNATELY, WE ARE LOST."

(For a moment he is silent...you swallow hard...)

"Now the GOOD news: FORTUNATELY, WE HAVE PICKED UP A TERRIFIC TAIL WIND AND WE'RE MAKING GREAT TIME!" [1]

Sounds silly, doesn't it? However, many individuals navigate life under the same premise. It has been said that those who are not sure where they are headed seem to be in the biggest hurry to get there!

Many organizations are also carried on strong, swift winds with limited knowledge about a desired destination. What's the problem? Fuzzy focus.

Focus = Aim

Fuzzy focus often means lack of direction and destination. Unclear purpose. One synonym for focus is "aim." Aim for something concrete and you have focus. Identify your challenge and you have focus: a desired, designated destination. Focusing is the first and most important step in becoming decisive. Focusing provides a clear, crisp picture of what you intend to achieve.

Personally, I have two recent examples always foremost in my mind to help me remember the importance of a crystal clear focus.

New Eyes

The first happened on a Friday afternoon. September 19, 1997 at 3:30 p.m. in Sacramento, California to be precise! Obviously I will never forget the details because it represents a major life change, milestone and dream-come-true. To me it's almost magic.

I got focused. Literally.

At the Pacific Laser Eye Center, a surgeon positioned me under an Excimer Laser machine and a beam of light shot diagonally across the cornea of each eyeball, making an "X" pattern, reshaping the tissue and ridding me of the fuzziness which prevented me from focusing for all of my forty-three years of life!

After only twenty seconds for each swipe (a total of one minute and twenty seconds) I went from minus 400 to perfect 20/20 vision. There is no way to describe the difference this has made in my life. The first time I went swimming without worrying about hitting my head on the side of the pool or coming out of the water blind, I actually cried! The first night I woke up in the dark and could read the digital clock, I squealed!

Funny Focus

There are many funny and humiliating memories associated with thick glasses and hard contact lenses that had to be worn because I was nearsighted and astygmatic. One illustration is my first date.

I was born and raised in the Allegheny Mountains of Pennsylvania. No one had much money. So a date could be as simple as a walk in a field. Mine was. I was thirteen. Very pudgy. Well, fat. The boy's name was Tommy. He told me we would go for a walk on a sunny Saturday afternoon and that we would hold hands.

Very self conscious because of the heavy, horn-rimmed "Coke-bottle" glasses everyone teased me about, I decided not to wear them. Tommy and I were walking through the field. In my mind we were gliding. Floating. I had a date! I was wearing my prettiest cotton dress. All of a sudden I wanted to do something romantic I had seen on a TV commercial. I wanted to jump up on a tree stump.

I imagined Tommy putting his hands on my (big) hips and helping me down and gazing into my big brown eyes.

"What did you do that for!" Tommy's horrified voice accented how stupid I felt as the soft, squishy "tree stump" gave way beneath me. I could smell it even as I reached into my purse for those ugly, old, cracked glasses.

What I thought to be a tree stump was a huge, brown, fresh cow pie! EEEYEEEWWW! I managed to free my used-to-be white pumps from the suction-like hold they were in, turned and ran home, never to speak to Tommy again! What a difference a clear focus would have made to a young mountain girl!

Distracted or Deliberate

Before relating my second example, I want you to know an idea about the absolute importance of focus that came to me from the PRKa surgical procedure on my eyes.[2]

The folks at the center were meticulous about educating patients and preparing us for surgery. We had to watch a teaching video. We had to read and study a manual. We had to listen to audio cassettes. We had to take written tests.

After everything we learned, one thing was drummed in to our heads about the actual seconds under the laser beam. It had to do with focus. It had everything to do with being deliberate and not distracted.

The Red Light District

"The surgeon will operate the machine," we were enlightened about the intricacy and reliability of the equipment. "The anesthesiologist will place one drop of numbing liquid in each eye," patients remain awake during the short operation.

"Your only responsibility is to focus on a bright red light that will be in front of your eye during the procedure."

My understanding was that if I would dart my eye during the process, the Excimer Laser Machine would shut itself off and abort the transaction. Otherwise, the eye would be misshapen. Wow, did I want to focus.

I usually like to joke and laugh and try to make the doctor laugh when I'm having out-patient procedures or dental work done. Maybe it calms my nerves. Would I be able to just stare at a red light?

As Doctor Meister gently positioned my head and his assistant clamped my eyes open, it occurred to me that I didn't have to operate the machine, or put drops in my own eyes, or make sure the floor was clean or answer the phone or even drive my car home.

The doctor, assistants, receptionists and my husband would take care of everything else. All I had to do was focus on the red light.

"Red Light. Red Light. Red Light." I was chanting inside my head. I have to admit there was this strange temptation to look quickly to the right or left, but something began to fascinate me. The big, fuzzy reddish-pink blur became clearer, closer, crisper and redder with every click of the machine! I could see!

Marcel Proust wrote:

> *The real voyage of discovery consists*
> *not in seeking new landscapes*
> *but in having new eyes.*

Application:

Distractions are tempting and keep us from focusing on our goals. Distracted people worry about what others are doing. Deliberate people stay focused on their own goals. Distracted people look around. Deliberate people look ahead. Distracted people compare and want to always BE the best. Deliberate people confront and want to always DO their best! Distracted people spin. Deliberate people win!

Make Three Columns:

Title the first one **Deliberate** and under it list no more than four decisions you need to make or goals you are longing to reach. Be very specific. Remember that someone said "a goal is a dream with a deadline." Try to pencil in a realistic deadline beside each goal or decision. These are in pencil because deciders know things change. Change does not concern a decisive person. Accepting change is part of being a confident, charactered decider.

The next column should be **Action.** Under it write one action you need to take to help you make a final decision or come closer to a goal. The other column should be entitled **Distractions.** List obvious distractions that keep you from being focused.

After you have done this, take a blank sheet of paper. Begin to write down realistic and practical ideas on eliminating specific distractions.

Narrow Your Focus

Try to be very specific about every decision you make starting right now. For example, instead of saying "I want to get a job." Think about what is really important and specific to you. Then add on more specifics and narrow your focus. "I want to do something I love, support my family, live in Michigan, use my skills, work only with people who inspire me, keep my life in balance, improve the conditions of those I serve, make enough money to cover vacations and retirement years."

Maybe your decision has to do with getting healthier or more physically fit. Be specific. Do not cop out by being general. Instead of saying, "I want to lose weight," or "I want to be healthier," add on: "I want to fit comfortably in the expensive business suit hanging in my closet, mow the lawn without puffing, jump rope for 10 minutes without collapsing, participate in a triathalon next May."

Congratulations if you are making a decision to be more decisive! To narrow your focus, just keep asking yourself one question: "Why?" The answers may sound like this — "I want to be more decisive so I can save time, live without regret, stop worrying about what others think, quit second guessing myself, see more results, grow my business, make more money, have more control..."

Look back at the four potential decisions you wrote down under the **Deliberate** heading. One at a time ask yourself the question, "why?" as many times as you need to get a clear, sharp image after each item. Write the answers down on a separate sheet of paper for each decision. Begin to narrow your focus until you know specifically what you are after.

Cultivate focus-ability. Like the red light my eyeball needed to zero in on, your goal must be brightly in front of you. As you deliberately concentrate on it, your purpose — like my red light — will become less fuzzy, more crystal clear.

Difficult as it may seem, resist the urge to allow a plethora of choices to distract or disturb you.

Be Careful: Controllers & Wimps

And here I have a word of caution I will mention again and again. Deciding just for the sake of deciding is meaningless and sometimes manipulative. On the other hand, *not deciding IS deciding.* Is that confusing? Let me explain.

Dominating Deciders

Control freaks fire off decisions on everyone's behalf. Every time her sisters get together for a vacation, Janette decides where they will go. She doesn't like to eat out, so they stay at a condo with a kitchenette complete with stoneware dishes that have to be washed. Janette plans menus, assigns chores and insists everyone takes a turn cooking dinner.

Not wanting to rock the boat no one challenges Janette. She thinks everyone is happy. They are not. Her decisions are meaningless in the long run, manipulative in the short run, and the sisters have given up their right to choose.

Not Deciding IS Deciding

Refusing to make a decision or waiting too long to make one ends up being a decision! Usually the wrong one. Darcy finally had enough money for a down payment on a victorian house she loved in the city. Rent payments were draining her and so was the long commute to work. She put off her decision because out of town guests showed up for the week end.

Then she put it off a little longer because she had to catch up on some projects. Her reasons for putting off making an offer on that house, which was a really great deal, were not even relevant or well thought out. She didn't say, "Oh, I'll wait and see if interest rates drop," or "maybe I like this other place better."

By not deciding, Darcy made a decision. Someone else submitted an offer and escrow closed for them thirty days later.

Deciding To Wait Is OK

Deciding by default is different than deciding to wait to decide. Kurt had a job offer in the midwest. It was with the same company he worked for in Virginia. After gathering information, he decided to wait, setting a self-imposed deadline of ten days to make his decision because he felt the need for more time to weigh benefits and drawbacks.

In the meantime, the northern California office had an opening. Kurt had always wanted to work in California and he was qualified. He got the job and in retrospect is happy he decided to wait to decide!

By waiting for proper timing, some decisions don't need to be made. For instance, we went to Greece in March. Months before, when making travel arrangements, I began to think about what to pack. Predictably the weather would be very cold. Heavy coats were in order. Fortunately, I was too busy at the time to give it unnecessary, advanced concern.

As it turns out, I checked the Internet a week before we left and Athens, Corinth, even the Island of Mikinos was having unseasonably warm weather. Packing was simple. It worked itself out.

Micronesia?

Remember I said there was another story? My second example and reminder of the importance of focus in addition to eye surgery was a surprise trip to the tiny island of Ebeye. (Pronounced eeeeBYE).

I was speaking at a conference in South Lake Tahoe in the springtime last year when a phone call came for me. A conference meeting planner had tracked me down. Five different sources had recommended my name as a presenter for an association in the Marshall Islands. The conference would be held on the Island of Majuro.

"Will you go?" Hank Jones asked me.

"I might consider it," I answered, "If I had even the slightest idea where it is!"

Purpose And Focus

Know where you're going. Sounds simple. But remember the DC 10 story? It does not matter how efficient you are, how fast you are moving, how good you are at your trade, if you don't know the destination.

Roy Saunderson, in his book *How To Focus On Success!*, relates his motivating personal story about destination and purpose. He clipped a newspaper article about a new hospital that was to be built. A wing with a rehabilitation facility was part of the plan. Roy tacked that clipping to his bulletin board. He was still getting an education, but dreamed of serving individuals wrought with spinal cord and brain injuries someday. He wanted to work, not just anywhere, but in that particular location.

Five and a half years later the same newspaper clipping was still pinned to the same cork board, keeping Roy constantly focused on his destination. Overcoming self-doubt, hard work, long hours and many challenges he landed his dream job.

That faded little piece of paper gave Roy Saunders a purpose, focus and sure direction.

Inspiration

A favorite quote that kept Roy inspired is by Henry David Thoreau:

If one advances confidently in the direction of his dreams and endeavors to live the life which he has imagined, he will meet with a success unexpected in common hours. [3]

I also have a quote from Thoreau that has inspired me to rid myself of distractions. Maybe it will help you:

I had three pieces of limestone on my desk, but I was terrified to find that they required to be dusted daily, when the furniture of my mind was all undusted still, and I threw them out of the window in disgust. [4]

Where Am I Going?

Internet surfing helped me find the Marshall Islands. They, 1100 tiny "atolls" are in Micronesia, half way between Australia and Hawaii in the South Pacific. Eight more hours of flying and I would have been in Guam.

After learning as much as I could about my destination, Majuro, to my dismay the conference location was changed at the last minute to the very tiny atoll, Ebeye. It is one mile long by three blocks wide. In one spot it's only about a block wide!

"Will you still come?" Even over the phone we needed translators. I had a tough time finding information about Ebeye with such short notice. In the end, had I known where I was going I probably would have stayed home! I'm glad I didn't. I spent eight days on that tiny South Pacific piece of land with three interpreters and many wonderful Marshalleese people. My life is much richer from the experience and I am planning to go back to them again next year.

Those little islands became a symbol for me. A three part symbol about knowing where you are going and making your best decisions every time. (See figure 1).

In figure one you see that the words Purpose, Mission and Vision form a triangle or the tip of an arrow pointing to the future.

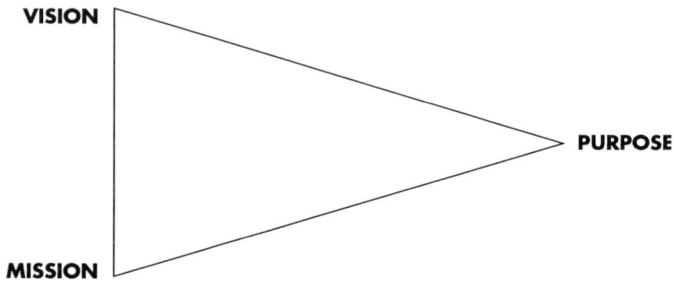

(Figure 1)

Chapter three will contain details for making a purpose statement, a mission statement, and a vision statement. Important exercises for decisive people. Right now take note that:

1. Purpose = Destination
2. Mission = Map
3. Vision = Vehicle

My Destination was to land at a military base, Kwajalein, and then sail to Ebeye. I downloaded a photo from the Internet. I also printed out a map. While the photo was great to have, it didn't give me instructions like the map did. But more detailed and important were the two airplanes and the boat that actually carried me to my goal.

Decision-making is a lot like that long trip of mine. You need a purpose (destination), a mission (map, written instructions or directions) and a vision (the actual vehicles, the details to launch, carry and land you at the destination). If a goal is a dream with a deadline, a vision is a dream with details. To come up with a vision you must explore your options. Read on.

Summary

❑ Being decisive is the most important change you can make for a successful future.

❑ To be decisive you must first learn to FOCUS. To FOCUS means to identify your challenge.

❑ Choosing to be deliberate rather than distracted will cause you to narrow your focus and become more decisive.

Copy or clip this and post it where you will see it daily:

Distracted People:	Deliberate People:
1. worry	2. focus
3. look around	4. look ahead
5. compare with despair	6. confront with confidence
7. want to BE the best	8. want to DO their best
Distracted people spin! —	Deliberate people win!

Two Fundamental Laws
Of Decision-Making

I.

Everyone Will
Not Applaud Your Decision

II.

Decision Minus Action
Equals Delusion

Basic Rules For Being Decisive

1. Never spend unnecessary time on necessary decisions.

2. Time, effort and thought invested in any decision should be proportionate to the magnitude and long term significance of that decision.

3. Get as much input as possible, but not more than you can digest. Gather information. Know when to stop.

4. Have foundational values in place. Never violate your moral code of ethics (this will take care of at least 85% of your decisions).

5. Pray, Plan & Proceed. Your own rituals for making decisions will help you to become comfortable and confident.

6. Review your purpose-mission-vision often. (See chapter three, "CHOOSE.")

7. Get and stay organized. Eliminate the URGENT! from dominating your life.

8. Force yourself to keep all necessities and repetitive activities simple. When the decision is mundane, adopt a "this will do" policy.

9. Remind yourself often that virtually all decisions are subjective. Know yourself. Have confidence in your innate ability to decide for the best.

10. Practice "turn-the-page" discipline. Once you have made a decision, resist the urge to go back and re-read your script. Move on to a new chapter.

11. Don't buy into the deception that one decision will make or break your private life or your business. Some of the world's most successful people made and lost fortunes over and over again.

How Decisive Are You?

Choose your probable response to the following situations:

1. You go to a movie and love it. The next day you read reviews in a major newspaper and the best known movie critics give it a thumbs down. You:

   a. decide not to tell anyone you saw it.

   b. tell people you hated it and quote the reviews.

   c. tell people you liked it, but apologize for disagreeing with the reviews.

   d. tell people you liked it and why you did.

2. You are job hunting and after four interviews you instinctively know you are a perfect fit for

company #2. Numbers 1 and 3 phone you with job offers but give deadlines for your answer. You:

a. Take the first job offer for fear of ending up empty-handed.

b. Ask for the #1 and #3 deadlines to be extended.

c. Phone the company you like and confidently request a time line, letting them know you believe you are a great fit.

d. Combination of b and c.

3. How difficult is it for you to delegate responsibility to others?

a. I feel I'm shirking responsibility when I delegate.

b. I make all the decisions because I want to be in control.

c. I have a hard time choosing someone else for a task and anyway, I can do it faster myself.

d. Delegating gives me the opportunity to mentor others as well as prioritize projects.

4. Do you make lists?

   a. Never

   b. Sometimes

   c. When it's convenient

   d. Daily

Types Of Decisions We Make

Ethical Decisions
Employment Decisions
Enjoyable Decisions
Emergency Decisions
Life-Changing (Attitude) Decisions
Mundane Decisions
Medical Decisions

Quiz Results:

"D" Answers Indicate:

If your answers were mostly or all "D" answers, you are on your way to being a very DECISIVE person!

A-B-C Equals F:

If you answered in the a,b, or c category all or most of the time, you need to work on decision making skills.

You also need to work on confidence in your ability to decide. Read on...

TWO

EXPLORE

I know why mug-wumps avoid decision-making. Deciding is risky. Every single time you do it, you run the risk of being wrong. Of course, you also have a wonderful opportunity of being right. Either way, however, deciding seems to me less frustrating than having to live in that self-imposed state of paralysis known as decidophobia... I'd just as soon go the wrong direction now and then, as never go anywhere.

— Calvin Miller [1]

EXPLORE

I have heard that Henry Ford once refused to hire a man because he saw him sprinkle salt on his food before tasting it. Apparently Ford, the industrialist who "put America on wheels" and became the world's richest man when he was 40, believed his employees should, unlike that man, be individuals who gather facts and explore options before making a decision.

Four Components

In this chapter I want to talk about four ways to explore options. Ideas for making the best decisions are gathered through experience, knowledge, wisdom and moral fortitude.

1. Searching for ideas: EXPERIENCE

Carly Fiorina's bright face graced the cover on a recent issue of FORTUNE magazine. According to the article inside, Fiorina is number one on a list of "The Fifty Most Powerful Women in American Business." To put this in perspective, Oprah Winfrey is named number two.

I was at a Lucent Technologies conference in Scottsdale, Arizona the day that issue of FORTUNE hit the newsstands and it was exciting to be in a room full of people jazzed to have one of their own recognized and celebrated.

Fiorina, a 44 year old "supersaleswoman," as the article reports, runs the core business of Lucent Technologies which is the largest telecommunications equipment company in the world. Her division's sales in 1998 were estimated at $19 billion.[2]

Getting There

How did she arrive at such lofty heights? You might think she meticulously planned every move from day one in kindergarten. Wrong. Apparently at one point her father said he didn't think she'd ever amount to anything.

Carly Fiorina said her original dream was to become a classical pianist. Instead she went to law school because her father wanted her to go but dropped out because she did not want to go. She became an English teacher in Bologna, Italy. After that she got a job with AT&T.

You might say Fiorina is an extreme example of someone who knew how to explore options! She took the scenic route to her dreams. "A funny thing happened to me on the way to being recognized as America's most powerful business woman!" she might say.

The University of You

Most of us wouldn't do it her way because those are not OUR options. What Carly did right was to build on her unique character qualities, skills and experiences. She has a knack for seeing an opportunity in every problem.

Problems are only classrooms in the university of experience. Experience is the greatest teacher or learning center of all time. Just think, Sam Walton did not have an MBA. He built the Wal-Mart empire with an abundance of people skills, sales savvy and what some might call a master's degree in the school of experience.

We all have our own private university if you think of it that way.

Many successful business people reached their pinnacles through experience — some experiences are perceived by others as failures. I once interviewed Howard Putnam for a newspaper article I was writing. He gave me a great perspective on this.

Putnam became CEO of Southwest Airlines in 1973 and is credited with creating the most successful and most people-oriented airline in history. Later he was recruited to navigate Braniff International "into, through and out of Chapter 11."

The Braniff fiasco was a tough ordeal. But Howard Putnam still does not categorize it as failure. Details were daily plastered on newspaper headlines.

Howard has a hilarious story from that time period about encountering a stranger who was griping and complaining until he asked, "And what do you do?" When Mr. Putnam told him he was Chief Executive Officer for Braniff, the guy exclaimed, "And I thought I was having a bad day!" Many thought Putnam was crazy for taking a nose-dive job with Braniff.

Regret is a Robber

The Winds of Turbulence is the title of a book Putnam wrote about how to thrive on the "cutting edge of corporate crisis." Howard told me he believes there are great decisions and tough decisions but no such thing as a regrettable or bad decision.

"Regret robs us of energy," he said.

"Critical situations create their own urgency...In order to endure and overcome crisis, people need new information, new skills, and new paradigms for understanding and action," he wrote.

Howard says successful people

1. Inform
2. Educate
3. Act decisively.[3]

Decisions are a summary of all that we have experienced and all of our training. Aldous Huxley wrote: "Experience is not what happens to a man. It's what a man does with what happens to him."

Experience for Hire

Experience is our own best private tutor. One day an employee at IBM made a mistake that cost the company $600,000. CEO Tom Watson was queried as to whether or not he was planning to fire that employee. His answer was, "No! I just spent $600,000 training him! Why would I want somebody else to hire his experience?" [4]

After focusing on a challenge and narrowing that focus, searching for ideas through experience can be important.

2. Searching for ideas: **KNOWLEDGE**

Thomas Edison failed thousands of times before finally perfecting the electric light bulb. It is said that one day an employee came to him, discouraged, because a project failed.

"Mr. Edison, it cannot be done. It just won't work," the young man lamented.

"How often have you tried?" asked Edison.

"About two thousand times," replied the worker.

"Then go back and try it two thousand more times," said Edison. "You have only found out that there are two thousand ways in which it cannot be done."[5]

That employee had information. He needed to turn it into knowledge.

Our Age

We live and breathe in the "information age." But information is different from knowledge. Information becomes knowledge when it is relevant to circumstance. In other words, if you can marry data to a decision you need to make, it becomes knowledge. As we will see, the key to surviving under the avalanche of information today is application, not volume.

Overinformed, Overwhelmed

I just made a telephone call to the DISH Network™ System. They informed me that they have 300 television stations. I'm not sure anyone knows exactly and the numbers are changing daily, but the last I heard, including other satellite and cable systems, we are approaching a total of 500 television stations where there used to be only three major networks. When I was a little girl in the 1950's we did not have a TV.

Just from TV alone we can obtain an avalanche of information, data, entertainment and junk. Information rains on us from everywhere. I read an article in the Sacramento Bee last year that documented the thousands of times a business person is bombarded and interrupted by messages and information during an eight hour day. (I clipped the article, but I have saved so much information and data that it has apparently drowned in my sea of words. Maybe I will resuscitate it before I finish this book.)

Pagers. Beepers. Buzzers. Doorbells. Telephone bells. Intercoms. Call Waiting. Call Forwarding. Answering machines. E-Mail. Web Sites. Federal Express & overnight mail. Snail Mail. Star Six Nine. Faxes. Modems. Laptops.

You've Got (too much) Mail!

Each year 63.7 billion pieces of third-class mail find their way into mail boxes across the nation. The average American professional will spend eight entire months dealing with mail solicitations during his or her lifetime. For each adult, an average of 41 pounds of junk mail are generated every year. It's estimated that 39% of all U.S. mail is third-class, weighing in at 4 million tons per year.

Tell me, is unsolicited mail information or knowledge? Or just an irritant?

The last time I was in Hawaii I waited two days before retrieving my voice mail messages. I had twenty-two! There was a time early on after subscribing to an Internet service when I was excited to hear that cheery and now movie-famous phrase: "You've got mail!"

Nowadays, knowing there are probably a dozen or more hits waiting for my response, when I fire up the hard drive and modem, I am not as easily thrilled. When I traveled to Ebeye, I carried my Zenith laptop computer with me. Guess what? Ebeye did not have individual telephones connected to the modern world! And they only had electricity six hours a day. I survived and the planet progressed without benefit of my outdated 14.4 modem.

Deciders are Users

Confident deciders use technology instead of allowing it to use them. They sift data and move easily into and out of the information age prison. For instance, a few years ago we had a freak snow storm in Cameron Park, which is only 30 miles east of Sacramento. Our power failed and we were stuck with unplowed roads, happily boiling hotdogs and tea on our woodburning stove and storing milk in snowdrifts to keep it cold when the refrigerator wasn't. If you're reading this in Minnesota, Chicago or Pennsylvania, you're thinking, "Big deal!"

I have a 1910 Royal typewriter. What an experience when I was desperate enough to sit at the kitchen table, banging away on those heavy keys, trying to get my thoughts down! But our family enjoyed every minute of the snowball fights and telling stories by the light of a candle and flash light each evening and the universe of data glut marched on without us.

After a power outage I put the antique Royal in storage, crank up my word processor, make phone calls & faxes on one line and check E-Mail on the other. A garden of options! I love and can live in both worlds. Anytime I need to shut down or close the office, I can pretend there's a snow storm.

Paradise or Prison?

Please hear this again: confident decision-makers do not become slaves to technology. They are ones who choose to see the age of information as paradise instead of prison. They understand that it is impossible to exploit every opportunity or take advantage of every option. Instead of attending time management seminars to learn about doing more in less time, they do less, but more of the right things.

I weary of hearing business people, speakers, entertainers, news anchors, homemakers, just about everyone whine about how modern technology has extended the work week. Because we can be reached 24 hours a day some people never shut down or turn off. But they CHOOSE to never have down time. Since it is their choice, why should others have to listen to them whine and complain about it?

One speaker said, "Few people would describe our modern day as a technological paradise." Guess what? Here's a person who does. I was recently encouraged by a friend's example. She lives in Moscow and many people want to keep in touch.

Last week I received e-mail as did many others in our network informing us that time constraints prevent her from immediately responding to the mountains of greetings she receives, and she asked us to be patient when waiting for a reply. Modern technology allowed her to send that brief message once, by clicking one button, to many hundreds of recipients.

Unlike my friend, many people stress out, trying to answer every message and interruption. Life for them becomes a side show spinning plates.

Let Your Burglar Answer

While channel surfing one day I stopped to watch a gripping scene in a dramatic movie. In retrospect, this is a sad and absurd example of how some people are slaves to technology.

In the movie, an intruder bursts into a woman's apartment and tries to kill her in the middle of the night. The music swells as she breaks away from his strangle hold and smashes a vase over his head. Scrambling and shaking to save herself she climbs out a window on to a fire-escape complete with a ladder reaching to the ground below.

Whew! I'm thinking, *She made it!*

But – UH-OH – what's that ringing? The telephone. The camera focuses in on it. Then on the girl hanging out the window. Then on the burglar. In the dark the viewer can see him regaining consciousness.

The woman, you guessed it, climbs back in the window and answers the phone. When she said "Hello?" I changed the channel because I couldn't bear to find out what would happen to such a stupid individual.

I hope it has occurred to you that you don't always need to answer the phone. Even if you don't have burglars, it's no sin to use God's gift of modern technology: Voice mail. Get a machine. Get a life. That way if there is good information you can turn into knowledge, someone will leave a message and you can harvest it.

Otherwise it may be a telemarketer like the one I chatted with yesterday who was so persuasive he sold me eight more TV channels for my satellite dish programming!

Finding Information for Decisions

Where do you find the kind of data to translate into knowledge when researching a decision? I spoke with author Jeff Davidson today by phone. He reminded me that this year there will be 155,000 books published in the United States. Did you realize that just one Sunday edition of the New York Times newspaper contains more printed information than an average person living in the 1800's would have been exposed to in his or her entire lifetime?

Information is everywhere:

❏ Libraries

❏ Internet Sites and Web Pages

❏ Experts in Person (Teachers, Professors, Authors, Celebrities)

❏ Bookstores, New & Used

❏ CD Rom Libraries

❏ Encyclopedias

❏ Your Mom

❏ Your Dad

Erma for Info

I once wrote a letter to Erma Bombeck and enclosed two pages of questions and a self addressed stamped envelope. Graciously she answered each question on her old electric typewriter! Erma's personal response proves that you can get the information you need if you persevere. Regularly I visit used bookstores. There is a wealth of wonderful information on every subject you can imagine. New mega bookstores and small, cozy neighborhood bookstores and bookstores on the Internet are exciting for any topic you need to research.

A Garden Paradise

I like the funny poem about knowledge that must have been written by one of those young people in the 1800's who didn't have the New York Times on Sunday:

How nice 'twould be if knowledge grew
On bushes as the berries do;
Then we would plant our speller seed
And gather all the words we need
And sums from off the slates we'd wipe
And wait for figures to be ripe,
And go into the field and pick
Whole bushels of arithmetic.

Or if we wished to learn Chinese
We'd just go out and shake the trees,
And grammar, then in all our towns
Would grow with proper verbs and nouns;
And in the garden there would be
Great bunches of geography,
And all the passersby would stop
And marvel at the knowledge crop.[6]

Information is everywhere. All the time. Right at your fingertips. But is it knowledge? That is for you to decide. If you can use it to enhance your business or personal life it is.

3. Searching for ideas:
WISDOM

Roger Dawson, in his terrific book, *The Confident Decision Maker* relates an old story of a hotel in San Diego. The hotel had a problem: No elevator and no room for an elevator. Quite a few expensive engineering consultants were hired to solve what they saw as an insurmountable dilemma. As the consultants stood in the lobby discussing the matter and probably rubbing their chins and scratching their heads, (and being paid by the hour), a janitor approached them.

"Why don't you just put an elevator on the outside of the building?" he asked, matter of factly.

Although they were shocked to note not one of their own highly educated employees had conceived of an outside elevator, the janitor's exhortation was seriously considered. You know the rest of the story. Now outside elevators are a common sight in every city.

Outside the Boundaries

Wow! It's OK to color outside the lines. It's acceptable to think outside the box. Even outside the building. This is wisdom verses knowledge.

Education, information and knowledge may be at our fingertips in this "information age." However, failure to use it all properly is a lack of wisdom. For knowledge to be translated to wisdom it must be used in a timely manner. It must be wedded to opportunity.

Data + Circumstance = Knowledge

Knowledge + Timing = Wisdom

Wisdom + Breathing = Experience

Experience + Knowledge + Wisdom + Moral Fortitude

Equals Your Best Decision Every Time!

What's the Difference?

I once heard a teacher explain the difference between knowledge and wisdom very effectively:

When you are walking down a country road and you see a black kitty cat with a white stripe running down it's back and recognize what it really is – that is knowledge.

When your brain says "Move!" and you do before he does – that's wisdom.

Three qualities of wise decisions are:

❑ Timing

❑ Opportunity

❑ Scale

Timing: "GO!" or "NO-GO!" decisions often must be made on the spot, using intuition and past experience. Say you want to invest in real estate. Several bids have come in on the property you want. Make your move now or forever hold your peace. (And let go of your piece.)

For other decisions, timing means "Don't rush." I used to be a great worry wart (many, many years ago). When I started implementing time saving techniques into my life, I started keeping worry lists and worry files. They save time. Let me explain.

On my nightstand was a pad & pencil. I called it my worry list. If I woke up in the night troubled about something, I would simply pencil it in (not even turning on the light) and then forget about it. I was so busy from morning to night at that time in my life that the only uninterrupted interval for thinking something through was about forty-five minutes, very early on Sunday mornings.

That was my designated worry list time. I simply looked at that list during the designated hour and that way I didn't forget to worry about anything! Amazingly, everything took care of itself, minus the worry, and I slept every night!

Now I use file folders. Recently I accepted a speaking engagement in Santa Cruz, a business trip to Chicago and a leadership commitment in Sacramento. Two of them are 15 months into the future and one is almost two years away.

File folders with dates and topics, contracts and

suggested themes in chronological order in my oak file chest take those future commitments off my mind and free it up for today's tasks and pleasures. Tickler files keep track of ideas I don't want to forget. As the calendar spot approaches, I'll add data to the file folders, schedule in some preparation time and when the event is upon me, I won't have a thing to worry about.

Here's one of my pearls of wisdom I often share at seminars: **Guilt drags you into the past, worry sucks you into the future, and they both cause you to miss hope which anchors you in today.**

Guilt Drags You Into The Past

Worry Sucks You Into The Future

Hope Anchors You In Today

Decisive People Choose To Live In Today

Opportunity: The ability to recognize an opportunity and not miss it is the greatest timing of all. Imagine being a person who got in on the ground floor of Microsoft or Yahoo! I have never purchased a lottery ticket, but perhaps you could assume that the winners were in the right place at the right time.

If you ever stayed at a Hilton hotel you probably received a complementary paperback biography of Conrad Hilton's life. He was not looking to become the owner and operator of a lucrative hotel chain. In fact, the day he bought his first hotel he was in town on other business. He just happened to be in the right place at the right time. He recognized a problem (his failed business deal) and found an opportunity (the hotel).

He took a risk. He made a decision. The rest is history.

Scale: All decisions are not equal. Bring your big guns out for big decisions. For instance, company projects that could be milestones for your department. Whether or not to move corporate headquarters across the country. Choosing to hire a dynamo for the marketing department.

Research big decisions. Glide through small ones. Gather information. Know when to stop. Recently I was on a business trip in Pocatello, Idaho. Lunchtime at a popular restaurant found me seated near two indecisive women.

They combed the menu, summoning the server again and again to ask about portion sizes, prices, variations in the configuration of specials, dessert options, payment plans, stock options...irrelevancies. They talked ad nauseam about menu items and choices, never making a choice.

Who knows? They may be sitting there still! When I left they had not made one selection! They looked stressed out. Over a luncheon menu! Since lunch is such a daily event, we must classify it in the less important classification of decision making. A large number of our everyday decisions belong there.

Most Important Decision

The most important choice a decisive person must make is what to measure in life. What deserves precious time, effort, study and thought? When should I bring out my big guns?

Which hill is high enough to die on? Here's an example of what I'm talking about. Until July 1996 Sam Maselli served as a government affairs representative and legislative aide for a member of congress in Washington, D.C. Now Maselli is the executive vice president of WRTA (Western Rural Telephone Association) in Sacramento, California. When Maselli took the position with WRTA it was headquartered in Santa Rosa.

Why did he move it? He researched alternatives, opportunities and possibilities and came to some compelling conclusions.

"Sacramento is the third largest town for trade associations in the country with a talented pool of potential employees."

After focusing on his challenge and exploring other western cities, he made a choice. The scale of this decision required time, work, mental aerobics and risks. Maselli is happy with his decision and seeing it pay off in a growing and profitable organization.

Maselli says, "Never second guess yourself. You never benefit by wavering. And when you do make a decision, the most critical thing is to support yourself. Get what you need to implement your decisions."

Rule To Remember

Never spend unnecessary time on necessary decisions. This brings timing, opportunity and scale together. The least important decisions require the least amount of time. Set some foundational minimum standards for inconsequential, low level decisions. Then choose the first alternative that comes along and meets with your minimum requirements.

For instance, if you need to buy napkins and the store has hundreds of colors to choose from, buy white and get on with your life. The goal is to quickly choose an item, freeing yourself to decide other things. We make hundreds, maybe thousands of decisions a day. Many can fit into this manageable, minimum standard classification.

When we make a habit of this practice our decision making expertise increases. Our goal is to BE DECISIVE! We'll also have more time to look for ideas and collect knowledge for medium and high level, more important decisions.

4. Searching for ideas:
MORAL FORTITUDE

Good for Business

I recently spoke to a group of managers during a ninety minute presentation about why ethics is good for business. I could have spent another ninety minutes talking about why the absence of a moral compass in the workplace can lead to poor decisions and destroy a business. One sensational example of this was the shocking demise of Barings Bank at the hands of one unethical employee, Nick Leeson.

Barings Bank was a "centuries-old global institution of solid reputation." [7] Trading fraud in the amount of $1.7 billion brought this well-respected company of solid repute into bankruptcy as Leeson's improprieties were made known.

The Whole Truth

Moral fortitude is principled resolution. I would estimate that 85% of our decisions are related to practices of integrity. Honest wages for honest work. Honest representation of business practices. Telling the whole truth, not just a fraction of it. Billing practices. Integrity on an IRS tax form.

Commitment to ethical practice makes the deciding process smooth and can pay off big in the short and long run. In the telecommunications industry I once heard a manager say that of six potential suppliers, five privately promised him technology that was not even invented. One honest supplier said, "Frank, I would like this job but I'm not going to tell you I can provide equipment that doesn't even exist."

The manager shook his hand and hired him because he already knew the others had given him a line about what they could do, trying to impress him. In other words, they were dishonest.

Most companies establish core values to guide their business practices. Surfing the net will give you some good ideas. Here is a statement I found by Jean C. Monty, President and CEO of Nortel:

Acting With Integrity

"As an operating principle, we will conduct our business honestly and ethically wherever we operate in the world. Acting with integrity builds credibility – that fragile, intangible asset that's so hard to gain, so easy to lose, and so difficult to regain. Ethical conduct is the way we protect our credibility as a company, establish respect for the dignity of every individual, earn the trust of our partners and customers, and define the character of our business."

Consider this information from the Ethics Resource Center in Washington D.C. In a survey of 4000 employees:

- ❑ 33% felt pressured often to violate policy
- ❑ 50% felt pressured once to violate policy
- ❑ 33% witnessed the following unlawful acts:
  - ✦ 56% lying to supervisors
  - ✦ 35% stealing and theft
  - ✦ 35% sexual harassment
  - ✦ 31% drug/alcohol abuse
  - ✦ 31% conflict of interest

From the book, *The Day America Told The Truth* employees confidentially admitted to:

- ❑ 50% calling in sick when they are not
- ❑ 50% receiving wages for 5 days when they work only 4
- ❑ 16% admit using alcohol or drugs on the job
- ❑ 70% say they are not loyal to their company
- ❑ 90% say they are not happy with their jobs[8]

Shula-kinda-guys know the answer

Where does moral fortitude originate? Why do some employees cheat? Why do some supervisors and managers decide to become unfair and dishonest? Why do sales people and suppliers decide to misrepresent their products? Why do individuals decide to exaggerate? Why do politicians decide to lie?

Some circles of commerce place a taboo on any reference to faith. Not so in sports. Sacramento's largest newspaper recently ran a large article on Randall Cunningham, quarterback for the Minnesota Vikings. In every paragraph he mentioned his faith. He was not censored. The big talk this year has been how Cunningham decided to leave his tile-laying business and return to playing football.

Everyone seems fascinated with how he made that life altering decision. He makes no apologies for believing God led him. He has been given quite a forum to express his faith. Another sports figure, Don Shula, moved into the business world when he co-authored a book with Ken Blanchard. *Everyone's A Coach* is the title.

Coach Don Shula led the Miami Dolphins to five Super Bowl appearances and the Baltimore Colts to one. *Sports Illustrated* calls Shula the "winningest coach in sports history."

Blanchard asked Bill Arnsparger, former Shula assistant and one of the greatest defensive coaches in the NFL what made Shula great.

"Don is great because of the decisions he has made. And the decisions he has made have been based on his religion. His faith has made him the tremendous person he is."

Moral fortitude, ethics, foundational faith. Whatever you call it, that's what makes the difference. It is a necessary ingredient in the practice of being decisive.

The following pages contain self-awareness exams and rules to consider in the A-B-C's of ethical decision making.

BE DECISIVE! in the marketplace. Make all decisions based on moral fortitude and integrity.

Summary

- ❑ Explore options to make your best decisions. (Don't salt your food before you taste it!)

- ❑ Experience, knowledge, wisdom and moral fortitude must be cultivated, combined and practiced if you want to BE DECISIVE!

- ❑ Don't spend unnecessary time on necessary decisions.

- ❑ Decisive people know what to measure in life. Don't bring out big guns for small decisions.

- ❑ Timing, Opportunity, and Scale all play a part in successful decision-making.

Eight Step Quiz for Making Ethical Business Decisions

1. **Is it lawful?** If the answer is "no" stop right here. Legal, lawful, the right thing to do – it all means the same thing. Make it very clear: *We are not going to break ANY laws here. Ever. Period.*

2. **Is it consistent with our company values of honesty, fairness and integrity?** To comply with company values you must make them widely known. Post them attractively in restrooms, near refreshment stations. Establish a 24 hour hotline where employees can seek advice or vent issues in a non-threatening way or where they can simply ask a question about policy.

3. **How would it look as a headline on the national evening TV news?** Imagine your decision as a front page news story. Imagine your plan being sent out over the company E-Mail system. Imagine what you thought about doing, or not doing – blaming someone else for your mistake or not giving due credit for an idea – being made public. If you're uncomfortable with that. Change plans.

4. **Do you have all the information you need?** Some violations have more to do with ignorance than with ethics. Get ALL the facts.

5. **Would you tell your mother you did it or your child to do it?** Don't laugh. Imagine telling your mother proudly "I figured out a way to have my employees work overtime without being paid." Or imagine telling your nine year old son, "I had someone else write a presentation and did not give him or her credit." If your mom or child would not be proud of you. Stop.

6. **Are you asking the right questions?** If you are ever unsure, ask and keep on asking. Don't carry all the pressure yourself. Get input from co-workers. If something feels wrong, solicit advice from human resources or another supervisor or a confidential counselor.

7. **Are you taking enough time?** Some unwise decisions are more a result of hastiness than lack of values.

8. **Does it need to be covered up?** Revelation builds trust.

Benefits Of Ethical Behavior
In The Workplace

1. Employee Empowerment Due To Self-Regulating Work Environment

2. Increased Productivity Due To Time And Money Saved

3. Loyalty And Corporate Confidence

4. Longevity: Less Employee Turnover

5. Creativity Fostered In Stress-Free Atmosphere

6. Knowledgeable Workers And Strong Teamwork Due To Mutual Trust

Other? _____

_____

_____

_____

_____

_____

Causes Of Unethical Behavior In The Workplace

1. Pressure To Produce

2. Ignorance Of The Law

3. Being *Value Driven* Instead Of *Ethics Centered*

4. Self-Protection

5. Self-Promotion

6. Power Brokerage

Other? _____

_____

_____

_____

_____

_____

_____

A B C's of a Corporate Ethics Program

AWARNESS LEVELS INCREASED

• instill confidence that employees are informed about the law or legal codes with which they must comply.

BUILDING BLOCKS FOR A RELIABLE PROCESS IN PLACE

• encourage reporting of ethics violations or ethics commendations.

• use a twenty four hour hotline or standard paper form or confidential counselor or other?

CREATING A SELF-REGULATING WORK ENVIRONMENT

• publish a simple policy handbook for easy reference, clear guidelines and workable tools.

• model and reward ethical decision-making.

Self-Awareness Test:

1. Am I aware of guidelines so I do not violate them?

2. Are my co-workers and subordinates aware of guidelines so they do not violate them?

3. How am I communicating policy, guidelines, values and procedures?

4. Do I set an example by behaving ethically 100% of the time – even when no one is looking?

5. Do I keep confidences? (This builds trust)

6. Am I fair in treatment of others?

7.   Do I take responsibility for my actions?

8.   Do I set clear consequences for questionable actions? Then implement them fairly?

9.   Do I believe in "moral compassing" and do I use it to judge all situations?

10. Do I understand the difference between "values" and a "moral compass"? Explain.

THREE

CHOOSE

Choices determine habit
Habit carves character
Character makes the big decisions

– Eleanor Doan

———————

Time flies, but remember:
You are the navigator.

– LAS

———————

If time could be our servant
our lives would be sublime
but if we do not master it
we're only "serving time."

– Daily Bread

———————

Choose the best
Streamline the rest

– LAS

CHOOSE

We all have 86,400 choices to make each day. That's how many seconds are in 1,440 minutes or a 24 hour slot. The IRS reports that if you prepare your own taxes you have chosen to use 37 hours and 19 minutes on record keeping, 5 hours and 10 minutes to learn about tax laws and 5 hours and 59 minutes filling out and sending in a form.

More Time-Saving, Less Time

Americans have more time saving devices and less time than ever before. Microwave ovens, video cameras and VCR machines, personal computers with voice recognition, scanners and digital photo imaging. Answering machines with voice mail boxes so we don't miss messages, caller ID so we can avoid messages. Twenty-four hour convenience shopping and ATM self serve gasoline. Optional timers on appliances for convenience. Catalog and Internet stores with overnight delivery. No-frill airlines with no-waiting, ticketless travel. Virtual warehouses so we can avoid shopping malls. Virtual reality so we don't have to deal with – reality?

Be Careful

Time has replaced money as the modern currency. Yet few have mastered the art of investing time like they invest money. Time is one resource we cannot manufacture. It is non-renewable and does not collect interest for a greater return. We can't store it up.

If we're not careful, someone else will steal seconds and consume our choices about how to use our own time. Consider this:

❑ We are exposed to over 1500 commercial messages a day. (Billboards, TV commercials, Radio, Newspaper and magazine advertisements, circulars and unsolicitated postal service, Internet ads that pop up unwanted on the screen, telemarketing phone calls...)

❑ There are over 10,000 magazines published in America on as many subjects

❑ More than 100 sales catalogs per household are produced and distributed every year

❑ 6,000 radio stations and nearly 500 TV stations compete for the airwaves every day (there are hundreds of satellites in orbit competing for outer space)

Hinges of Destiny

Minute by minute choices are the hinges of destiny. A telling column by Richard Ford highlights concern about losing ourselves by default.

Saying goodbye to the moment: Bombardment of messages robs us of any time to reflect on events.

"Put simply, the pace of life feels morally dangerous to me. And what I wish for is not to stop or even to slow it, but to be able to experience my lived days as valuable days. We all just want to keep our heads above the waves..." [1]

Choosing to be decisive allows us to control environments. To paraphrase something Richard Foster, author of *Reasons to Be Glad* and *A Celebration of Discipline*, wrote:

The decisive person is the person who can do what needs to be done when it needs to be done. The decisive person is the person who can live in the appropriateness of the hour. The extreme ascetic and the glutton have exactly the same problem: they cannot live appropriately; they cannot do what needs to be done when it needs to be done.

The decisive person is the free person. [2]

Live Long; Live Smart

Current life expectancy for men is 72 and for women, 77. In the fourteenth century, the average lifespan was 38. In the nineteenth century it was 49. We are now living longer, but are we living smarter?

Several years ago a quick witted poet summed up the average life when she penned, "This is the age of the half-read page, and the quick hash and the mad dash, and the bright night with fluorescent lights and nerves tight, the plane hop and the brief stop, the lamp tan in a short span, the big shot with a good spot, and the brain strain and the heart pain, and cat naps till the spring snaps and the fun's done and taps sung. [3]

Zadig's Truth

Voltaire, the famous Frenchman asked: "What of all things in the world, is the longest and the shortest, the swiftest and the slowest, the most divisible and the most extended, the most neglected and the most regretted without which nothing can be done, which devours all that is little, and enlivens all that is great? (A question put to Zadig by the Grand Magi in, *Zadig, A Mystery of Fate*.)

The answer? "TIME":

"Nothing is longer, since it is the measure of eternity. Nothing is shorter, since it is insufficient for the accomplishment of your projects. Nothing is more slow to him that expects; nothing more rapid to him that enjoys. In greatness it extends to infinity, in smallness it is infinitely divisible. All men neglect it; all regret the loss of it; nothing can be done without it. It consigns to oblivion whatever is unworthy of being transmitted to posterity, and it immortalizes such actions as are truly great. Time is man's most precious asset." [4]

Can We Talk?

In the next few pages, let us invest our time in a discussion of how to become more decisive by taking charge of our choices. Choosing is the third step we must climb in each decision making endeavor. Focus. Explore. Choose. Step. Step. Step. Move to the top.

Making a habit of making the best decision possible every time requires a constant practice of:

1. Selective Bridge Burning and Building

2. Prioritizing Priorities: Purpose – Mission – Vision

1. Making Choices:
SELECTIVE BRIDGE BURNING

What to tell Jay Leno

Imagine being contacted by Jay Leno. You are invited to be on the Tonight Show. He wants you to sit in that famous chair beside his desk. He is going to ask you questions in front of millions of viewers. He wants you to tell your story. "Yes!!" Who wouldn't say, "Yes!!" ?

"No." That's what Ada Williams Lee said to Jay Leno's producers in 1998 when they asked her to appear on NBC's top rated national television talk show.

"The thought of being on TV, of being limousined around L.A., merely made Miss Ada chuckle," her friend, Donna Britt wrote. [5]

Can you imagine? You probably could if you knew Ada was 107 years old. She was once courted by her future husband in a horse and buggy. Still laughing, lucid and involved in the world, Ada felt free to say no to an opportuntiy others would see as obligatory. It's OK to say "No" when you have more important things to do.

Who determines what is important in your life? It's between you and your Maker. And when the two of you decide what's important, be ruthless about attending to it. Pulitzer-prize winner, Annie Dillard advises would-be writers to go at their lives with a broad axe. [6]

A woman I greatly admired, Miriam Adeney, author of *A Time For Risking* once told me she gave up playing the violin and sewing clothes for her family, both activities she greatly enjoyed, to pursue writing, speaking and pursuing her calling.

Most women advance in years before they realize that "No" is a word as beautiful, useful and active as "Yes."

The goal of bridge burning and being very selective about bridge building is balanced living. Three practices have helped me immensely.

Yes and No

1. When you say "Yes" to something, make sure you also say "No" to something. It only makes sense. Thoreau said no to limestone and tossed it out the window. He was saying yes to dusting his brain!

If you say yes to working at the office during lunch, you are saying no to having lunch at the Plaza. If you say yes to grocery shopping you are saying no to the gas station. Do the same thing every time opportunities present themselves.

When your boss dumps another project with an unrealistic deadline on your desk, speak up. Show her the other projects you are working on and ask her to choose the priority. Experience the joy and abandon of throwing your expertise full throttle into a project. You might never overbook again. And you may start doing prize-winning work.

When the phone rings and you are being roped into taking a board position for the PTA or the NSA or the PGA or the Rotary or Lion's Club or Meetings Industry Council, stop. Look at your calendar, your work schedule. Can you say "NO" to something else?

Ada said "No" to Leno. She said "Yes" to spending time with Joe, her 83 year old son. (I adored Donna saying that by the look on his face when Ada went to heaven very recently, anyone could see that even 83 years is not long enough to be loved by a mom.)

Eighty Per-Cent

2. Another way to select your bridges and choose is to fill your life up 80%. This creates mega breathing space and can be practiced everywhere.

Only commit 80% of your calendar to the future. Leave some of those squares blank. It is amazing how dates will fill to capacity with unexpected events as they approach. Put eight things on your daily list instead of ten. Do them well.

Fill your closet up 80%. You can almost hear your clothes breathing. When you travel, leave space in your suitcase. Imagine the joy of finding room for the chenille scarf you bought in Venice and the book you purchased at the Louvre.

Clutter or Cluster

3. Here's an elementary tip for freeing up brain molecules, leaving margins for better pursuits: Put like things together. One of the biggest barriers to making powerful decisions is confusion and clutter. Instead of cluttering, try clustering.

Did you know that a four drawer file cabinet is designed to hold 18,000 pieces of paper? Even so, when you are looking for data, it should not take you longer than 30 seconds to find it. This should be true of everything in your life. The key to surviving an avalanche of information is application. Can you access the items you need when you need them?

In your office, keep similar supplies together, close to where you need them. Store everything according to color and size. In your closets store clothing according to color. When you are working on a presentation or several projects, don't cross pollinate! Doing so leads to confusion, clutter and will keep you from being a decisive person.

Carving Elephants

In chapter one we talked about focusing in on a challenge. We all have more than one challenge at a time begging for decisions and commitments. And we constantly try to balance competing time demands.

Forcing ourselves to focus on one challenge at a time and narrowing that focus leads us quickly to the second step of exploring options. In chapter two we talked about where to search for ideas. When we find them, we must categorize and then limit options.

We must sculpt a plan. We must choose. A woodcarver's nephew admired the beautiful animal statues his uncle produced with a whittling knife and some choice pieces of oak.

"Uncle," he asked. "How do you carve a horse?"

"Well, boy, You just knock off everything that doesn't look like a horse!"

I giggled at a Dilbert cartoon in our local paper with that same idea, different twist. He is standing in front of a raw chunk of marble, chisel in hand, musing that someone told him to sculpt an elephant you just knock off everything that doesn't look like an elephant.

In the end, broken pieces of marble are scattered at his feet and the pedestal is empty. "I guess this chunk of marble did not have an elephant in it," he laments.

Norm Crampton said, "Disposal is the handmaiden of an orderly mind."

To choose the best, streamline the rest.

2. Prioritizing Priorities:
PURPOSE – MISSION – VISION

(See figure 1 in chapter one: Focus)

Popcorn & Apples

Make a habit of prioritizing every possession, person, project, and responsibility in your life everywhere, on an ongoing basis, all the time.

A wide-mouthed glass jar filled with popcorn kernels and plastic apples decorates my desk as a reminder that life can be balanced if I put first things first.

Try this. The apples are the kind you hang on a Christmas tree. They are for sale in craft stores. They remind me of the important fruit of living – priorities. Five such priorities top my list. God, Family, Career, Service to Others, Self. If you have five apples, or golf balls or whatever, place them in the jar first. Now pour popcorn over them until the jar is completely full. Put the lid on.

Try reversing it. Popcorn signifies all the little things in life. They scream for attention, but they are not eternal fruit. If you put the popcorn in first, the apples won't fit.

Maybe two or three of them will. But which one has to go? Usually for women it's "Me." No time to exercise, eat right, pray, think. Sometimes it's your spouse or kids that get neglected and left out. Or for some, career suffers.

And, don't forget, if you could apply enough heat, the popcorn would blow up and you would have no room at all for any of the most important stuff: the sweet fruit that makes life worth living!

Life is like that. Everything can get blown out of proportion and take more time than calculated when heated up by stress. Popcorn stuff in my life is some of the repetitious, mundane, irritating or difficult ongoing responsibilities. Commuting by car or plane to work. Packing for travel. Grocery shopping. Mopping grape juice off the kitchen floor. Giving the dog a bath. Dealing with unwanted body hair!

There's always something calling for attention and there always will be. The art of prioritizing is knowing which voice to heed. The secret of success here becomes evident only when you have a life purpose.

Finding Your Purpose

George Gallup, Jr. conducted a poll to determine preeminent needs of the average American. Topping the list were:

1. The need for shelter and food
2. The need to believe life is meaningful and has a purpose
3. The need for a sense of community and deeper relationships
4. The need to be appreciated and respected
5. The need to be listened to and be heard. [7]

Knowing life has purpose is ranked right after staying alive. This seems to be a popular theme. I watched a national TV news magazine show featuring the parents of an ill baby. The parents, knowing their infant daughter did not have long to live, were planning to participate in the organ donor program.

"At least we will be assured that her life had meaning and purpose," they told the host.

Even someone as viable and popular as Oprah Winfrey has been heard saying she does not want to live her life and miss the purpose for which she was sent to earth. Purpose is powerful as a motivator. Purpose is important to determine. How do we do it?

Purpose = Destination

All you have to do is determine your destination. Norman Rohrer was my first writing mentor. He is the president of the Hume Lake Christian Writers Guild and his letterhead says he lives in "The Write House." Norm gave me a writing assignment.

"Write your epitaph," he said.

But he didn't leave it at that. "Telescope it down to as few words as possible."

For me, that became a challenge. I started paying attention to epitaphs because it was obvious that to choose one would be a decision about my life purpose. My destination. Where I wanted to go. My epitaph would sum up my life, "telescoping" it into a few words. Here are some I found:

The body of B. Franklin
Printer
Like the cover of an old book
its contents torn out
And stript of its lettering and gilding
Lies here food for worms.
But the work shall not be wholly lost
For it will, as he believes, appear
once more
In a new and more perfect edition
Corrected and amended
By the Author.

I thought the "food for worms" part was lovely.

Someone quipped: Better a little "taffy" while they are living than so much "epitaphy" when they're dead.

Here's a sad one:

This man died at 30; he was buried at 70.

Here's an original inscription which someone amended later:

Remember, friend, when passing by,
As you are now, so once was I.
As I am now, soon you will be,
Prepare for death and follow me.

Someone came along with a sharp object and carved an added comment to that one:

To follow you I'm not content
Until I know which way you went.

One person said,

"My purpose in life is
to become the person
my dog thinks I am!"

Marketplace Purpose

It wouldn't be a bad thing for business owners to think of writing a purpose statement. Two questions can yield a bottom line answer.

1. If I heard two people in the seats behind me on an airplane talking about my business and how it affects their lives, what would I hope to hear?

2. Years into the future if people came across a statement about me or my company, what would I hope to know they are reading?

Breakfast of Champions

Think about this. Wheaties cereal wants to be known as the "Breakfast of Champions." If there was such a thing as a cereal epitaph, that would be it. "Wheaties is the breakfast of champions" could be recognized as a simple purpose statement for that product. It defines General Mills desire for recognition from consumers.

In a previous chapter, I mentioned my trip to Ebeye. That was my final destination, thousands of miles from my starting point at the San Francisco airport. The closest place with an available aerial photograph was Kwajalein. I downloaded it from the internet and it served to help me focus on my destination, my purpose for the trip.

Rubber Shoes

It took me months to settle on a personal epitaph. Years later I am comfortable with and even defined by my epitaph. Sedona, Arizona was where I discovered it. Our family was at Rock Slide National

Park. This must be where the idea for commercial waterslides originated for there are miles of smooth rock with rivers of clear water rushing over them to create a slippery ride.

Rubber soled shoes are required because the look of the rock is deceptive. It appears solid, but years of buffing by tons and tons of rushing water have made it slicker than black ice. At the end of the day, I was sitting on a low bridge at the bottom of the run with my feet in a clear, shallow lake of water. I noticed a man and his two sons walking toward the pool in front of me and they were not wearing the required shoes.

Before I had a chance to warn them, the man stepped into the shallow rock-bottomed water and I heard a sickening thud as his skull cracked on the rock. Without even a thought I picked him up swiftly by the shoulders. Already a thick stream of blood was swirling down around his neck.

The Bondage of Self-Absorption

I pulled some of his thick black hair apart to expose a one inch gash. You know how head wounds bleed.

"Here, give me your hand." I told him to pinch the gash together and that I would take him to the first aid station. However, his sons took over and as they walked away my own teenaged son, Dustin, let out a wail.

He was looking at me, horrified, as I stood gloved in a stranger's fresh blood. Dustin knew I had cut my finger earlier in the day and you can imagine what worried him. The potential of HIV infection.

"Mother! You come and wash your hands immediately!" he commanded. And as I watched the blood draining off my fingers under the faucet, my eyes clouded over to think that maybe we live in an era where we must be so concerned with self-protection we can no longer care with abandon for fellow human beings.

That's when my epitaph flashed before my eyes. For I realized I was committed to something powerful.

Self-protection can be a prison. Self-absorption can become bondage. Caring frees us from the prison of self-protection. That's a noble purpose.

Hopefully if you stumble across my tombstone some day it will have two words on it:

Lou Ann Cares

Creating Purpose

You can have a purpose statement for any project or product you are working on. You can have a purpose statement for your business, your career. You can create one for your family.

When you are creating a personal purpose statement, keep the following in mind:

1. A purpose statement is a destination. It is a short summary or description. Mission and vision statements become more detailed.

2. Consider your personality when settling on a personal purpose statement. Are you a "take charge" person who likes to lead the way? Are you an "idea" person who likes to motivate others? Are you a "meticulous" thinker who likes to organize and get things as perfect as possible? Are you a "paced" person who never burns out because you like to accomplish projects a bite at a time rather than in a whirlwind?

You could summarize the four personality types this way:

a. **Do**   b. **Think**   c. **Motivate**   d. **Pace**

This will help you in many decisions. Shortly after I settled on an epitaph and sent it to Norm to complete my writing assignment, I had to consider whether or not to accept an invitation to attend a conference in Dallas.

When the information arrived in the mail, I learned the theme: "A Heart That Cares." I decided to go because of that, and the networking opportunities proved to be extremely fruitful in my life and work.

Assignment:

1. Write the purpose statement for your life, your business, a product or a project you are working on.

2. Telescope it into as few words as possible.

   Personal _____

   Business _____

   Project _____

   Product _____

   Plan _____

3. Ask at least three people if they agree with your purpose statement.

4. Try to construct a purpose statement for every major decision. Answer,

   • What do I want to accomplish by this decision? What is the destination?

   • What would the tombstone read if a decision or project could have one?

   • What would I hope to hear others saying about this decision or project?

5. Create a picture of the end result. If purpose is destination, then like my photo of Kwajalein in the Marshall Islands, and like the newspaper clipping Roy Saunderson had on his bulletin board, a picture of the results you are aiming for should help you head in the right direction.

Mission = Map

USAA® United Services Automobile Association, headquartered in San Antonio, Texas, makes sure clients have copies of their mission statement:

USAA®

OUR MISSION

To facilitate the financial security
of our members, associates and
their families through provision of
a full range of highly competitive
financial products and services;
in so doing, USAA seeks to be
the provider of choice for the
military community.

And they are! Writing and publishing a mission statement is like making a map when you want to be sure and reach your destination. Who doesn't? Who wants to be lost, traveling in circles? I'm sure Moses did not pre-plan forty treks around Mount Sinai.

"Without clearly drawn maps to the future, the organization remains hamstrung by the past," wrote Calvin Miller. [8]

Can You Get There From Here?

From all the options you have, your mission statement is a way of planning and choosing the best route. Mission statements are a way to BE DECISIVE and get where you want to go!

Charles Garfield said "One's mission is bound by no preconceived limitations. It inspires people to reach for what could be...It aligns personal ambition, job and organization, preserves health and family, and is grounded in...values to equal the basic qualities that used to be known in less ambiguous days as character." [9]

Workshop

Stephen R. Covey has developed "A Mission Statement Workshop" and published it in Appendix A in his book *First Things First*. You would do yourself and your career a good service by purchasing his book and completing the workshop assignment. He has included sample mission statements written by some of his clients.

One of my favorites is: "I will maintain a positive attitude and a sense of humor in everything I do. I want to be known by my family as a caring and loving husband and father; by my business associates as a fair and honest person; and by my friends as someone they can count on. To the people who work for me and with me, I pledge my respect and will strive everyday to earn their respect. Controlling all my actions is a strong sense of integrity which I believe the most important character trait." [10]

Here is a simpler example: "My mission in life is to be kind and generous and respectful to my family, friends and co-workers. I desire to help those in need when I can and be a role model and mentor, giving of my time and talents when possible."

Onesimus

Personally, my mission statement was inspired when I read the story of a runaway slave and a wealthy landowner. Onesimus was the name of the slave and he became friends with a prisoner who just happened to know his former owner. The prisoner wrote a letter on behalf of Onesimus requesting his freedom and in it he said, "your love has given me great joy and encouragement, because you, brother, have refreshed hearts." [11]

So I wrote, "My mission in life is: To give JOY. To give ENCOURAGEMENT. To REFRESH HEARTS."

I believe a mission statement can be simple. It builds on a modest purpose statement and grows towards a vision statement which is more detailed. A vision is insight with foresight. A vision is a dream with details.

Assignment

1. Write a mission statement for your life. Make it as long or short as you like. Most people have a paragraph or two. Or they use bullets or numbers from 1 to 10. Start with these words and fill in the blank:

My mission in life is _____

_____

_____

_____

_____

2. To help you in writing your mission statement, answer questions like these:

   ❏ Who is the most important person in my life and what do I admire most about that person?

   ❏ What moral character qualities are the most important to me?

   ❏ What gifts and talents do I have to offer in service to others?

   ❏ Where do I want to be and what do I want to be like in ten years? twenty?

   ❏ What is the most important decision I need to make today to become the person I want to be?

Vision = Vehicle

If purpose is destination and mission is map, then vision is vehicle. Every time you go anywhere these days you must consider the transportation. My friend, Suzy McMinn loves horses. She lives in the country. A horse could be a form of transportation for Suzy, but not for me.

Living in the city exposes you to taxis, bus lines, automobiles and sometimes underground metro systems. I could get to the bay area from Sacramento by train. Going to Hawaii? You'll need a boat or a plane. The transportation part of a trip is the nitty gritty detailed part. You must decide what's appropriate and what kind of fuel you need.

Blind Passion

Covey also writes an entire chapter about the passion of vision in *First Things First* and gives the topic much more attention and detail than I will here.

There is also power in vision. Helen Keller was once asked if she could think of anything worse than being blind. "It would be worse for me," she answered, "to have my sight, but have no vision."

Helen did not have sight but she certainly had the power of vision. John Haggai in Lead On! wrote: "When a group is under the direction of a person who has no vision, the result is confusion, disorder..." and Calvin Miller said, "Vision is the photographic image that guides a pilgrimage to the goal it depicts...Vision is a dream inebriated by imagination." [12]

If you have vision and you communicate it effectively to others, you will be a motivating leader.

> Vision + Communication = Motivation

Vision Grows

Your personal vision will grow out of your purpose and mission. Grasping a vision for life, business, ministry, family, marriage, recreation or any worthwhile endeavor often comes at an "Aha!" moment. Dale Carnegie had that kind of an experience and it changed his future for the better. In 1909 he lived in a bug infested apartment on West Fifty Sixth street in New York City.

He said in the morning he would reach for a neck tie from a bunch he had hanging on the wall and cockroaches would scatter in all directions. Every evening he would come home with a headache. He despised his job selling trucks and felt bitter when he realized the vision he had in college of being a writer had not turned into a dream-come-true, but a nightmare instead.

How To Win Friends

He decided to apply for a teaching job at a university but they turned him down so he ended up teaching adult night classes at a YMCA. That was when the future came to him. His students were not there for college credits. They had problems. They needed results. They needed practical, productive help.

Carnegie wanted to inspire his students, motivate them and help them. "I wasn't interested in making a lot of money, but I was interested in making a lot of living," he wrote later.

The textbook he developed for adult night classes in New York later became the best selling book, *How To Win Friends And Influence People.* It sold more than 30 million copies. And from the experiences of the people in his classes he conceived and authored the popular *How To Stop Worrying And Start Living: Time-Tested Methods for Conquering Worry.* It has been reprinted at least six times and sold over six million copies.

Carnegie developed the details of his vision based upon his original purpose or goal from college days. He desired to write and to speak. He wanted to inspire people and help them.

If he had given up or remained blind to his vision, he could have become one of those needy individuals he wrote about and helped. There is no way to measure how many men and women have been transformed by the writing, speaking and teaching of Dale Carnegie.

His legacy will linger and will continue to point people to their dreams. Robert Moskowitz wrote that "goals are the basic direction arrows of your life."

If you have purpose, mission, vision they will shape your daily goals and moment by moment decisions and will become well defined directional arrows pointing toward a solid, defined, fulfilling and profitable future.

Coeur d'Alene

My own vision statement is probably too detailed to interest you so I won't publish it here. However, I'll tell you that it came about from a couple of "Aha!" moments. One of them at Lake Coeur d'Alene, Idaho on the day my son started college at Cal Poly in San Luis Obispo. I was on a business trip with my husband, experiencing the very first moments of "empty nest."

I was so awed by the beauty of nature that I vowed to maintain a sense of wonder. To stay wonder-full I must be free and light. Bad habits and burdens can weigh me down. No matter how unsuccessful, I will never stop striving to be free from worries, striving to stay filled with the wonder of a green leaf, a caterpillar or a drop of water sparkling in the sun.

Or the 14th tee on the golf course at Lake Coeur d'Alene which floats freely on the lake!

Castles and Dreams

My other personal "Aha!" was on Cedar Ridge in Glen Erie, Colorado at a lone gravesite of a person

I greatly admired and who deeply influenced my life – but I never knew. I wanted to touch souls and help people like he helped me and millions of others with his words and life. That man even died helping others. He drowned when he jumped in a lake and saved someone else from drowning.

His epitaph, engraved on that solitary tombstone is, "No greater love hath any man than this: that he would lay down his life for a friend." [13] I sat by his grave, overlooking a majestic castle in the glen and listened, on my pocket cassette player, to a motivational talk he gave before I was even born! His name is Dawson Trotman and his talk was originally recorded on an old reel-to-reel electric recorder in 1952.

Dreary Day Box

One of the details of my vision statement is that "I want to touch a thousand lives in the next five years with JOY and ENCOURAGEMENT through writing and speaking." I didn't intend to count, but my files are filled with notes and letters from individuals who have become my friends because I have had the privilege of being a word-crafter. I have reached that goal and want to continue.

When I ran out of file space, I bought a trunk. I call it my Dreary Day Box because if I'm discouraged, I can reach in and find a letter to motivate me.

One letter came from a lady in the Philippines.

Someone brought American magazines to her village and she read an article of mine and wrote to say it changed her life! People have given me wonderful gifts and tokens of appreciation. Paintings hang on my wall. Last month a woman who makes unique dolls gave me one she could have sold for $300.00. To me it is priceless.

I've been able to travel and live my dreams.

Without a purpose, mission and vision statement written down, how would I have known whether or not I'm reaching any of my goals? If Dale Carnegie had not captured his vision and traded the job he despised for one he loved, he would not have been the only loser. When we follow our vision others will benefit.

Assignment

1. Dream of details for your vision.

2. Re-state your purpose and mission. Begin to add specific details. The more detailed, the better. Dates, numbers, places – nothing is too silly or unrealistic. No one has to see this but you.

3. Write a vision statement for your life, your job or an important relationship. Put it away for a few days and don't look at it. Change it as necessary in the future. Everything in life is subject to change without notice.

Summary

- ❏ Choose to invest time like you invest money: If Jay Leno calls, you can say "No."

- ❏ Only fill up 80% of your life. Leave some breathing space and margins.

- ❏ Choose to carve a horse: knock off everything that does not look like a horse.

- ❏ Construct a plan: Choose only one option.

- ❏ Work on Purpose, Vision, Mission and find direction in your life.

The Six Step "Be Decisive!" Exercise Plan

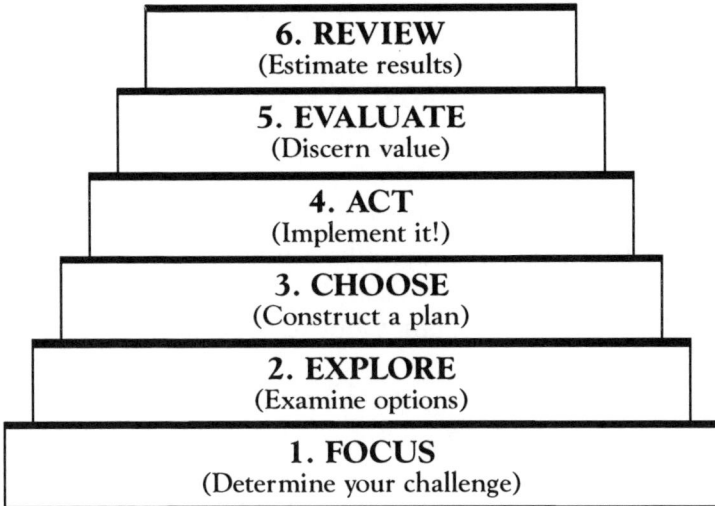

6. REVIEW (Estimate results)
5. EVALUATE (Discern value)
4. ACT (Implement it!)
3. CHOOSE (Construct a plan)
2. EXPLORE (Examine options)
1. FOCUS (Determine your challenge)

Step Up To Becoming More Decisive!

D.E.C.I.D.E.

D	Determine
E	Examine
C	Construct
I	Implement
D	Discern
E	Estimate

(Figure 2)

FOUR

ACT

You can't steer a parked car.
- Elisabeth Elliott

---

*Even if you're on the right track,
you'll get run over if you
stand there long enough.*
- Mark Twain

---

*When the pain of doing nothing
exceeds the pain of moving on,
you will move on.*
- Roger Dawson

---

*Our main business
is not to <u>see</u> what lies dimly
at a distance,
but to <u>do</u> what lies clearly at hand.*
- Thomas Carlyle

---

*Decisions without actions
are delusions.*
- LAS

ACT

*Take time to deliberate, but
when the time for action has
arrived, stop thinking and go in.*

– Napoleon Bonaparte

Dwight D. Eisenhower was in command on D-Day. It was his responsibility to activate "Operation Overlord," code name for the invasion plan. June 6, 1944 was the appointed time. Pictures of the French Coast taken from a Coast Guard landing barge that day showed thick fog and daunting surf.

Reports indicated Eisenhower nearly blew D-Day because he could not make up his mind on the best moment to attack. Finally he took action.

Courageously he gave the command, "No matter what the weather looks like, we have to go ahead now. Waiting any longer could be even more dangerous. So let's move it."

Being Decisive Means Being Proactive

Decisions without actions are delusions. Acting on right options with right timing determines destiny. How different might the entire world be if Eisenhower had waffled? Delayed action on right decisions gives birth to wrong decisions. And deciding to do nothing is deciding to do something.

For instance, if you plant a garden and you do not pull weeds you have decided to grow weeds! So, how did Dwight D. Eisenhower avoid that kind of mistake? How did he make his best decision on D-Day? He learned through years of training. He knew how to A.C.T.

Assess circumstances

Collect resources

Take off! Seize the moment!

Assess Circumstances: Two forty-nine year old men working for the same company are presented with the same option. Early retirement with an adequate but not overly impressive pension. One takes the out, the other doesn't. One has substantial savings and a real estate business on the side. The other has two youngsters in college and a second mortgage on the house. The first gentleman starts his own consulting business to supplement his retirement income. He and his wife are able to buy a new house and travel to Europe. The second individual stays with the company five more years. His kids graduate from college and are gainfully employed. He's considering an offer from another company in the industry. Who made the right decision? Both did. What was the deciding factor? Circumstance.

Collect Resources: We have already talked about exploring options. Resources are all around us. People are resources. Who is in your army? Eisenhower had capable soldiers ready to back up his decision. Information is a resource. Search for ideas. Nathan Myhrvold, Chief Technology officer at Microsoft, says, "Every day I have to make difficult decisions...I never make decisions in the thrill of the moment...I often make decisions in part by remembering what I've lived through. In other cases I draw on what I've read — whether it's about early Chinese civilization or the birth of the Renaissance in Italy." [1]

Take Off! Seize The Moment! If circumstances are right and you have collected resources don't let your decision decay. You may have a window of opportunity. Ron Evans says an "implementation gap" will "allow decisions to atrophy" and he sites examples of companies like General Motors and IBM who lost out to Toyota and Hewlett-Packard on big money makers because of inaction. [2]

The phrase "windows of opportunity" may bring to mind one of the most powerful decision makers of the last two decades. Everyone is talking about

Bill Gates. Last year he increased his wealth by $21.3 billion bringing his total to about $40 billion. He is way out in front as richest man in America.

"When I was 19, I caught sight of the future and based my career on what I saw. I turned out to have been right." says William Henry Gates III. His decisions were based on insight with foresight.

Risk

Strong decision makers have the ability to shoulder risk. Sister Helen Marie Schrift was my favorite teacher in high school. She also became a long time friend. One day when I was 15 and pudgy, pimply and insecure, Sr. Helen gave me a paper with a poem on it. I have kept it, shared it, copied it and recently noticed it in an inspirational book.

After reading that inspiring poem I wrote this in my sloppy, spiral English notebook:

> **"To live is to RISK,**
>
> **not to RISK**
>
> **is to RISK NOT LIVING!"**

Don't you think that's profound for a 15-year-old?

Here's the poem Sister Helen gave me:

To laugh is to appear the fool

To weep is to risk appearing sentimental

To reach out for another is to risk involvement

To expose feelings is to risk exposing your true self

To place your ideas, your dreams, before the crowd is to risk their loss.

To love is to risk not being loved in return.

To live is to risk dying.

To hope is to risk despair.

To try is to risk failure.

But risks must be taken, because the greatest hazard in life is to risk nothing.

The person who risks nothing, does nothing, has nothing, and is nothing.

He may avoid suffering and sorrow.

But he simply cannot learn, feel, change, grow, love, and live.

Chained by his certitudes, he is a slave.

He has forfeited freedom.

Only a person who risks is free! [3]

Dare to Decide

Triumphant individuals recognize risk. Without fear they move into challenges and dare to dream. And they don't put off dreaming and deciding. Stephanie Culp, author of *Streamlining Your Life*, says, "DECIDE TO DECIDE: Postponing decisions will only add to your problems, so decide to decide sooner rather than later. Continued indecisiveness will only turn into a snowball of consequences that can mow you down." [4]

I remember the first time we lived in a house with a swimming pool. No one told us about treating it with chemicals. For a while, we could not decide what to do. So, we did nothing. Do you think the water stayed crystal clean and clear?

You can guess. It turned green. Then a darker green. Then it turned brown and frogs came to live in it.

To live IS to risk. But consider the alternative. Decide to become more proactive today than you were yesterday. Appraise your unique circumstances. Collect and consider resources and information. Travel through the open window of opportunity to further opportunities.

An Excellent Decision

In the 70's Bill Gates did not have all the information about the future that could have assured him a perfect series of decisions, investments and successful risks. You will probably never have all the information you would like to have.

State-of-the-art is temporary as we approach the 21st century. Updated technology becomes outdated over night. New statistics are cranked out by researchers and journalists 24 hours a day. So, what if you don't have all the data to make a perfect decision?

Make an excellent decision instead. In this book we are not talking about making perfect decisions. There is a difference between perfection and excellence. We are talking about making the best decision every time.

Excellent decisions are the result of focusing on a challenge, exploring options, choosing one of those options, and taking the fourth step which is to act. Assess circumstances, collect resources and take off in the right direction.

Action is the tangible substance of a decision. Decisions without actions are delusions. By acting on our choices we learn to make better choices.

Cooking Lessons

Here's another way of seeing the need to translate circumstances and resources into action. Open a typical pantry door in a typical kitchen. Maybe it's filled with sacks of flour, sugar, eggs and all manner of cooking ingredients. Unless someone takes time and has talent to combine them into a recipe and bake, broil, grill or chill, packages remain as a bunch of useless stuff.

When's the last time you went to a dinner party and the hostess served a bowl of refined flour? Or a tablespoon of butter-flavored shortening and a raw egg?

Dreamed Up Data

A decision is only dreamed up data until it is acted upon. A good example was Dustin Hoffman portraying Ben, an indecisive young man in *The Graduate.* One morning he makes a well-received announcement to his delighted parents.

"I am going to marry Elaine," he mumbles without much emotion.

"Have you set a date?" they ask with happy anticipation.

"Oh, Elaine doesn't know anything about it," he answers.

Is This A Book Yet?

Everything works out in the movie for Ben, but his decision has no future until he acts on it. A lot of people have half-baked dreams. One example is ideas for books. Millions of people say "I am going to write a book someday." But how many actually do? Author Norman Mailer once set a goal of seven pages a day. That is about 1,750 words. At that pace you could have a book in about two months.

Ernest Hemingway kept track of his word count on a chart. He usually wrote 500 words a day. That's about two double-spaced pages.

When I started working on *BE DECISIVE!* the first step was an idea. Ideas are not concrete. When I began to collect data, articles, books, stories, newspapers and quotes it still was not a book. It was a dream with a deadline. When the pages started churning out of my Hewlett-Packard laser printer, it started looking like a book.

From idea to product the mortar in this project or any decision is action.

What keeps most people from acting on their good ideas? Here is a partial list:

REASONS FOR NOT MAKING A DECISION

- ❏ Fear of the unknown
- ❏ Fear of criticism
- ❏ Fear of failure
- ❏ Fear of success
- ❏ Fear of being wrong
- ❏ Fear of being laughed at
- ❏ Fear of making a mistake
- ❏ Lack of confidence
- ❏ Lack of information
- ❏ Lack of faith in God

❏ Lack of faith in others
❏ Lack of trust in their own judgement
❏ Lack of experience
❏ Procrastination
❏ Laziness
❏ Poor judgement
❏ Poverty of mind

When I say "poverty of mind" I am talking about people who see themselves as unworthy and undeserving. They are the ones who can never take a compliment. Someone says, "You look great!" and instead of graciously saying, "Thank you," they answer, "I look like trash."

"I like your dress."

"This old rag?" they moan.

The Lord said, "Blessed are the poor in spirit" not "Blessed are those with poverty of mind." To be poor in spirit simply means you have a sober judgement about yourself. In other words, you are sure that you are not the creator of the universe. You are also just as sure that you are gifted by your Maker and that your Maker wants to continue to bless you!

Larry Winget says you are God's gift to the world. What a wonderful thought. We are created as a work of art, worthy of all we were designed to be and do.

Worry is the greatest enemy of a good decision. Worry, it has been said, is a lot like a rocking chair. It will keep you moving, but never get you anywhere. When I am tempted to be frozen and atrophied by worry I pull out a quote by author, Corrie Ten Boom who wrote, "Worry does not empty tomorrow of its sorrow, it empties today of its strength. It does not enable us to escape evil. It makes us unfit to face evil when it comes. Worry is the interest you pay on trouble before it comes."

Worry is a cycle of inefficient thoughts whirling around a center of fear. Zig Ziglar says fear is: F-E-A-R, False Evidence Appearing Real.

You cannot make a good decision based on worry. "Good decisions are a magnet for wealth," Stedman Graham wrote in his book, *You Can Make It Happen.* [5] I had the privilege of writing an article for a national magazine that makes me believe Graham is right. It was about Harry Lahotsky. He lives in Winnipeg in a neighborhood dubbed "Murder's half acre" because the crime rate is so high.

Some think his decision is nuts. He has been criticized for raising kids in that atmosphere. However, his wife and kids are just as excited as he is about what they are doing. They are renovating old apartment houses that were once used for drug dealing and prostitution. Homeless people are finding homes. Hopeless people are finding hope.

Harry's life, commitment and attitude reminded me of Graham's comment, "Good decisions are a magnet for wealth." Not that Harry Lahotsky is a wealthy man by the standards of some. But that, too, is by choice. On a television news show, a business man was seen selling Harry a large building for one dollar. Others have done the same. Lahotsky donates the buildings to needy families and then other local businesses put up money and material to help with the projects. It's amazing. [6]

Risky? Yep. Amazing? Absolutely. Nuts? Who cares? Good decisions will absolutely attract whatever kind of wealth you are looking for. But first you must act on them.

How To Turn Decisions Into Action

A C T

1. **If you find a task too hard by the yard remember it's a cinch by the inch:** Break tasks down into do-able, chewable bites.

2. **You may have the newest shiniest Lexus in the neighborhood but if you don't take it out of "park" it won't take you to the park!** Do something! Don't procrastinate. It's impossible to steer a parked car.

3. **It is easier to act your way into a new kind of thinking than to think your way into a new habit of acting:** Behavior leads to believing. Act like you can do it. Stop making excuses.

4. **You would worry a lot less about what others think of you if you realized how little they do:** People are usually busy thinking about their own cares and are not obsessed with thinking about yours. So stop worrying so much about what others think.

5. **Eat healthy. Exercise daily. Die eventually.** So, do your best – pray it's blessed – give God the rest.

6. **We are all living constantly under the threat of apocalyptic catastrophe – that's why I just say "no!" to ironing.** Keep everything in perspective. Don't take yourself too seriously.

7. **Remember Tim Hansel's law of life: <u>Pain is inevitable but misery is optional</u>:** Choose JOY. You always have a choice. Decide for the best and remember, joy equals strength.

8. **Excellence is better than perfection:** The old saying, "If it's worth doing it's worth doing well" isn't true. Guess what? If it's worth doing, it's worth doing. Period. Just do something. Then do the next thing.

9. **Everything is subject to change without notice.** Get used to it.

10. **Living is risking.** Guess what the alternative is?

Summary

- ❏ Decisions without actions are delusions.

- ❏ Assess circumstances,

- ❏ Collect resources,

- ❏ Take off!

- ❏ There may be fog on the beach but go for it anyway.

FIVE

EVALUATE

Whatever you do, don't be like the person who said, "I used to be indecisive, but now I'm not so sure."

– Larry Winget

Balance is less about striving for some elusive state of equilibrium than it is about making an explicit series of choices in your life. You have to figure out what's important to you, and that's what will dictate how you spend your time.

– Dawn Gould LePore,
Executive Vice President and CIO,
Charles Schwab & CO. INC.
San Francisco, CA

EVALUATE

Margaret Harper, 44, attended one of my seminars. She wanted improved decision making skills and advice about scripting a better balancing act for life.

Margaret's career with a financial consulting firm is fulfilling. She also has a successful marriage which produced five beautiful children; three of them happen to be teenagers at the same time. In the midst of her busy life, Margaret H. made a decision.

Two years ago, with a little nudging from co-workers, friends and a college professor acquaintance, Margaret enrolled in night classes at a local university to acquire her MBA.

Balance and Choice

Apparently Miss Margaret said, "Yes" to college without saying "No" to anything else in her life and clearly she felt off balance. Even as we conversed she was on the verge of stress prompted tears.

Days at the office, evenings in class and week ends at the library suck away her energy. Her high schoolers are having challenges with assignments and her husband's job requires him to be out of town frequently so he can't always pick up the slack or attend parent-teacher meetings.

What should Margaret do? Does she have any choice? Of course she does. And you do. No matter how uncertain you may feel about past decisions or how fretful you may feel about future ones, right this minute you can become a better decider. In this chapter, let us explore how the next step in the BE DECISIVE! formula brings balance and makes even past decisions better.

Next Step: Value

After you 1)Focus 2)Explore 3)Choose and 4)Act, step up to 5)Evaluate. Step five, evaluating, is a good exercise for any decision you have made which is still impacting your life at the present time. Remember, every decision you have made has caused you to be the person you are and from this moment on, every decision you make will determine who you become.

The root word in the middle of "evaluate" is VALUE. When you evaluate a decision previously acted upon, you are determining value. There is value in every ethical action if made according to the best information available coupled with the highest intention. For that reason, you need never second guess or regret something you chose to do based on your finest motivation and intuition. This remains true even if the outcome was not what you predicted or hoped for. Even if no one applauds you.

It's Some Kind Of Life

Think about this example. In the 1940's Jimmy Stewart agreed to act in "A funny heartwarming fantasy about an honest, hardworking small town banker."[1]

Producers had high hopes for the film, but it was a dud at the box office. Critics said it was too long and too sentimental. What viewers wanted was the excitement and glamour of musicals and hilarity of slap stick comedy. The film lost money. The writers, producers and actors may have come to the conclusion that they should have never created it.

There was no such thing as a home video movie player then, remember? How do you think Jimmy Stewart felt as he had the joy of living long enough to see *It's A Wonderful Life* transformed into an absolute phenomenon? That simple, inspirational story is rated one of America's all time favorites. Who has not seen it? Even my son, Dustin, chose that as his favorite movie throughout his high school years. He did not even have a clue about who Jimmy Stewart or Donna Reed were.

No Regrets

Do not wipe away former decisions with second guessing or regret. You will be robbed of energy and joy. You will have less confidence in your ability to make great decisions in the future. Every time you act on a decision and every time you evaluate a decision, your judgement improves and you become a better decider.

When To Change Course

If decisions don't bring balance, hope, purpose or profit into life, change course. One entrepreneur I know composed a business plan, then set a date one year out for evaluation. She jotted down a simple formula for evaluation at that time:

High effort
High expense

No result

Change course!

Any effort
Any expense

Good results

Keep going!

Empowered by Choice

Our ability to choose and change is divinity in humanity. Put simply, choice is a powerful quality. Grasp and hold on to the realization that everywhere and always you have choices.

In *Man's Search For Meaning*, Viktor Frankl speaks of choice. In a Nazi concentration camp where he was enslaved, everything was taken away from prisoners. Forced labor and starvation ravaged their bodies. Looking back with a sense of tenderness and wonder, Frankl wrote years later about the deliberate choice he and others made to cultivate a sense of humor when they could.

They chose an attitude, the most personal and prized possession of a human being. Someone said, "Laughter is God's touch on a troubled world." An attitude of peace and joy is the greatest wealth life has to offer.

Freeing Decisions

Even in the stench and horror of death and hopelessness those abused men knew no one could rob them of dignity if they still had choices. So they made mild jokes like the ones about death camp soup and how they might act uncivilized at a dinner party if they were ever free again.

Other Nazi death camp survivors talked about choosing forgiveness as a form of empowerment and freedom. Unforgiveness is a big time waster.

> **Forgiveness Is**
> **Setting A Prisoner**
> # Free
> **Only To Learn**
> **The Prisoner Was**
> # Me

Bad – Good

Maintain ownership of your choices. If you don't make your choices, someone else will.

Seeing our own choices as positive and empowering strengthens us for the next challenge. However, we must acknowledge that there is such a thing as a bad decision. Every unethical decision is a bad decision.

In the must-read book for corporate America, *Heads You Win: How the Best Companies Think,* the authors poke fun at the world's first bad decision:

> The Judeo-Christian religious tradition can trace its roots to one incredibly bad decision made some number of years ago. As the Bible describes it, a serpent, with considerable marketing expertise, suggested a single alternative with an array of supposedly attractive benefits.

Adam and Eve bought the sales presentation and found themselves expelled from the Garden of Eden. That makes them the first decision makers on record to learn the dangers of failing to consider the adverse consequences associated with an alternative." [2]

Good – Better – Best

Some decisions are bad. But with perseverance, the right attitude, education and a little humor here and there all decisions can work together with other decisions and become good.

Think about that. Some decisions are bad. If you had a choice between going to choir practice and robbing a bank next Tuesday night and you chose to rob the bank, that would be a bad decision. (If you don't think so, you're reading the wrong book!)

We make hundreds of decisions a day and all of them can be categorized this way:

1. Bad or Good

2. Good or Better

3. Better or Best

4. Best or Very Best

5. Very Best or Very Very Best

To be a decisive person, you will want to live in category five and make your very best decisions all the time. You can. If your goal is to practice living and deciding in such a way that all bad-good-better-best options move out of the way and all you have left is Very Best, you can.

Good and Better: In the 1970's my husband and I had only $500 set aside in savings. We had the opportunity to purchase a three bedroom house in Sacramento for a rental investment. The advertised price was a little under $20,000. We practiced the focus, explore, choose, act process.

Then we borrowed enough money to add to our savings for a small down payment. A few years later the real estate market took off and we were able to sell the house for more than twice what we paid for it! There are a lot of "good" things you can do with five hundred dollars when you have two little kids running around the house. However, sound decision-making skills can lead to a "better" decision.

Better and Best: Building on confident decisions enables you to climb the ladder from good to best. What is best in one season of life may not be in another. Dawn Gould LePore was featured in *Fast Company*. She said until now she has chosen to fully focus on her career at Charles Schwab because it has been gratifying and challenging. Last year she chose to "change the equation" by having a baby. The change has made her a better delegator and less tolerant of activities that are not a good use of time.

Urgent vs. Important

One way to explain choosing very best over good is by explaining an exercise I was given by Jeff Davidson when I read his book, *Breathing Space*.[3]

I'm remembering this off the top of my head, but I think he said in order to get out from under the piles and piles of paper that cause information anxiety, and to become more organized with more breathing space in my life, I should make four stacks. Each would have a label. 1)Urgent! 2)Important 3)Interesting 4)Trash. Because I like alliteration I renamed my categories 1)IMPERATIVE! 2) Important 3) Interesting 4)Insignificant.

But back to Jeff's instructions. After labeling the four stacks, I needed to sort every paper in my world in to one of those piles and deal with it accordingly. Obviously URGENT! would be first.

Tyranny Kills Decisions

Many years ago I read a short booklet called *The Tyranny of the Urgent!* Impressed upon my brain was the idea that URGENT! is a negative word. The URGENT! will tyrannize me if I allow.[4] Being decisive is impossible for anyone refusing to conquer the tyranny of the URGENT!

Those who are always dealing with the URGENT! will never get to the important. They can never be decisive because the URGENT! will decide for them. I did not consciously recognize it when I started taking Jeff's advice, but my goal was to eliminate my URGENT! pile from ever existing again.

Happy to report: I have eliminated it completely. Now when organizing my desk I only have two labels: Important & Interesting. Perhaps they could also be called Very Best and Very Very Best.

Decisive Dumping

I have concluded that much of the information coming to me via E-Mail, Snail Mail or Voice Mail belongs to a practice Davidson calls "The Art Of Creative Trashing." I call it "Decisive Dumping."

Now when accessing mail there is a chant in my brain saying, "Do NOW; Dump NOW or File LATER." Do NOW means...guess what?...DO NOW! If someone requests a book or some marketing information or I get a letter from my sister or a contract for a speaking engagement and I intend to respond I may as well do it NOW.

Usually these tasks take seconds or minutes. Even though I work out of a home based office, I have a postage meter, photo copy machine and fax close to my computer and printer. Time saving devises help to eliminate the URGENT! If you are choosing to be a decisive person, make a commitment to acquire items that support your life and career choice. Otherwise you will try to operate in confusion.

For example, if you are a cobbler by trade, you want the latest state of the art equipment. How else will you grow and compete in your business? If you are an eye surgeon, you need the latest laser equipment. I read a disturbing article in the newspaper three days ago about medical doctors who are not keeping up with new technology and techniques and patients are being harmed as a result.

If I cannot or choose not to do some NOW activity, I place it in a vertical file at a work station near my desk. I regularly check this file because it only contains items that are time sensitive. Returning necessary voice mail messages within 24 hours and E-Mail messages on the spot further eliminates the URGENT! from becoming a horizontal monster pile.

Now I can live with the important. I can assign times and make appointments to read or write or work on a project in the important, interesting, "file later" piles. I am now deciding between Very Best and Very Very Best in my clutter control and papernoia arena.

Carried Over

This idea can be carried to all decision making. Here's how:

Remember Margaret? We left her stressed and tearful. She must eliminate the URGENT! from her life and decide what is important, interesting and desirable.

1. Admit that you do have choices. Never allow yourself to say, "I don't have any choice, I must do this or that." Instead say, "I **choose** to do this."

2. List every choice you can think of (especially the ridiculous ones, like Margaret could check in to a rubber room and weave baskets).

3. Affirm yourself in your choices. (e.g. "I chose to marry, to have these five wonderful kids, to go back to school. No one held a gun to my head to force me. I **chose** this life. And I love these kids, this job, this house...")

4. Ask yourself: What is important to me?

5. Ask yourself: Must I do this NOW?

6. Ask yourself: Must I do this AT ALL?

7. Ask yourself: If I knew today was my last day on earth, which activities, projects or people would get my full and undivided attention?

8. Implement the first four steps of the BE DECISIVE! process:

    a. **Focus** on your challenge, asking "Why"? so you can understand purpose, mission and vision.

    b. **Explore** options: Good, better, best, very best.

c. **Choose** one option.

d. **Act** on it by constructing a plan:

A

Assess Circumstances: What is happening in my environment that will support or prevent a decision I want to make? _____

_____

_____

C

Collect Resources: Name people, purchase tools and services, gather information and ideas to support you.

Resource people: _____

_____

_____

Ideas and Information: _____

_____

_____

Tools I have: _____

_____

_____

Tools I need to acquire: _____

_____

_____

T

Take Off! Take The First Step: Break your task down to manageable bites. Only name the very first step you must take to achieve your objective.

What I must do NOW _____

_____

_____

Look Back To Move Forward

Can you name the three most important decisions of your entire life? Write them down, with the date if possible:

My three most important decisions and when I made them:

1.

2.

3.

What did you see as three other options?

1.

2.

3.

What caused you to make each choice?

1.

2.

3.

Consider these questions: Would you change any of the three? How would you be different if you did? What value can you find in each choice? I can tell you without a doubt about my three life-changing decisions. To others they will not seem earth shattering or dramatic. Wealth is very subjective. Years ago a Picasso painting sold for $38 million. About the same time I read of a newspaper reporters encounter with Mother Teresa in Calcutta.

She was wiping pus and maggots from the sores on an old man's chest. He was lying in a gutter and the reporter who had followed her to get his interview covered his nose and mouth with a handkerchief to block out the smell of overpowering smell of death.

"Lady", he said in a muffled voice through the hanky, "I wouldn't do that for a million dollars."

"Sir," she said as she looked up at him briefly, "neither would I." Wealth was something very personal, subjective and spiritual to that woman. Wealth was more than millions of dollars. It was hitting the mark and valuing her purpose, mission and vision.

My three most important decisions in chronological order are: * Getting my first job at the United States Department of Agriculture in Washington D.C. * Becoming a wife and mother. * Finding peace with God.

The End of the Story

Margaret is fortunate to have supportive co-workers, spouse and family as part of her resource collection. She is delegating more. Cutting out some things by asking "Do I really need to do this? Do I really need to do it now?" She will continue working toward her degree and be her very best self because she evaluated the wisdom of all the quadrants of her life.

Her focus is becoming clearer and even though she told me choices will never be completely easy, she feels great recognizing that she is in the driver's seat.

Career coach, Laura Berman Fortgang, author of *Take Yourself to the Top*, says that to succeed in the future we must understand the power of choice and use it to peak advantage. Specifically, among other important advice, she tells clients:

❑ "Keep unacceptable things from building up in your life."

❑ "Live what matters to you most."

"You will no longer be planning your life and career, but rather designing them, truly letting choice be the palette from which you paint how you work and live." [5]

Summary

❑ Practice finding value in decisions. Evaluate means uncovering value.

❑ Eliminate the URGENT! or IMPERATIVE! from your life.

❑ Stop saying "I must." Instead say, "I choose."

❑ Continue choosing to live according to what matters not according to what happens.

SIX

REVIEW

It is clear the future holds opportunities – it also holds pitfalls. The trick will be to seize the opportunities, avoid the pitfalls, and get back home by 6:00.

– Woody Allen

A mistake is not the kiss of death. If you keep it in perspective, you'll be able to recover quickly, learn from the mistake, and move on.

– Julie Bick

Learn from the past but build to the future.

– LAS

REVIEW

We worship at the altar of overachievement then whine about being too busy. We pay homage to the gods and godesses of overcommitment then try to squeeze in a class on stress management and maybe one on time management. We claim to decide what is important but fail to live according to our decisions. We can't decide what to do next and end up doing nothing at all. Or at least nothing significant. Then we wonder at the fact that so many people are discontent.

Whacky Review

Roger Von Oech, wrote a polular book called, *A Whack on the Side of the Head*. Silly name, but some people seem to need one. In it, Von Oech shares this insight: "Life is tough. It takes up a lot of your time, all your weekends, and what do you get at the end of it? Death, a great reward. The life cycle is all backwards. You should die first and get it out of the way. Then you live for twenty years in an old age home, and get kicked out when you're too young. You get a gold watch and then you go to work. You work forty years until you're young enough to enjoy your retirement. You go to college and you party until you're ready for high school. Then you go to grade school, you become a little kid, you play, you have no responsibilities, you become a little baby, you go back into the womb, you spend your last nine months floating, and you finish off as a gleam in somebody's eye." [1]

Last Step, First Step

Von Oech's idea is a life review. I like it! Review means "to see again." Having a rear view mirror in your automobile enables you to look back while moving forward. Rear view mirrors in automobiles are such a good idea that the law requires you to have one. Too bad we can't install such a mandatory device in our brain to monitor a safe life and career journey.

What's going on in the other lanes on the highway of living? Are there unresolved decisions in our "blind spot"? Bad decisions that need to be corrected? Good ones that should be better? Better ones that can become our best decisions with a little effort? We hoped if we ignored them they would vanish. But the reality is, we might have a collision if we close our eyes to blind spots and fail to correct the course.

I laughed out loud when I read in this morning's paper that Senator Tom Hayden, Democrat in Los Angeles is introducing legislation to take legally blind motorists off the road. The bill will ban drivers license renewal for individuals whose corrected vision still leaves them in the dark.

Focus has everything to do with operating a motor vehicle on public streets. Remember, focus was the first step in the BE DECISIVE! plan. The last is to review or focus again on what did and did not work in the past so the journey to the future will be smoother and get you to your desired destination.

Your goal is to become a better decider.

Mistakes and Reviews

A crumpled up newspaper article holds a sacred place in my files. David McFarland wrote the piece in the Sacramento Union newspaper in 1991. In it he categorized mistakes.

1. Panic-Prompted: A decision made in fear, hurry and worry. Panic-prompted mistakes often show up in finance and romance.

2. Good-Intentioned: A decision with right motives, wrong methods. Good-intentioned mistakes abound in political moves, whether in office politics or government. Making money for your company is a good motive. Doing it unethically is a wrong method. Protecting a co-worker, spouse or constituent is good intention. Lying and cheating to accomplishment it wrong practice.

3. Neglect & Avoidance: A decision decaying from procrastination or lack of discipline. Writers often display this one and call it writer's block. It is characterized by missed opportunities and disappearing deadlines. An executive at a large technology firm spoke of a young employee who tried to use the old college crunch method of pulling all-nighters to get projects done. The result of waiting until the last moment resulted in poor performance and unfinished projects.

4. Blind-Spot: A decision made in ignorance. Stories abound regarding telemarketing scams which are a good example of blind-spot mistakes. A senior citizen receives a phone call from someone who offers investment opportunities, insurance, a luxury vacation or home improvement. The caller requests money up front. An uninformed victim loses life savings because of a blind-spot decision. Not taking time to explore options, gather information, and collect resources can result in this kind of error of judgement.

Look Up

I have paraphrased and amplified McFarland's classifications but want to give him credit for the basic ideas. Correcting course by looking at how we make decisions is an important part of the REVIEW step in decision skills. Do you have a blind-spot? Have you made panic-prompted decisions like taking the first job that came along? Are your intentions good but you're going at them the wrong way? Are you a procrastinator?

"Learn the lesson from that mistake so you won't have to go through it again," McFarland suggests. "And don't ever forget: Sorrow looks back, worry looks around, but faith looks up."

Ask the Right Questions

It's been said if you ask the wrong question you'll get the wrong answer. Here are some questions to ask yourself when reviewing a decision and planning on becoming a better decision maker.

1. Beat The Clock: Was this a time sensitive decision? Was I under pressure to make it? What would have happened if I had waited? Would more time invested have resulted in a better outcome? How can I avoid making panic-driven decisions from now on? Would scheduling in "think time" improve that type of decision when I must face one like it in the future?

2. Right And Wrong: Did this decision violate my own personal policy or company values? Did I have the necessary information to make an ethical decision? For example, IRS tax code knowledge helps you fill out the 1040 correctly. How does it make me feel when I make a decision that is morally wrong? Did I feel the need to make this decision because it made me look good or was profitable for me or my company? How must I prepare before I can effectively confront such a decision again? Is there a way to correct the wrong decision and make it right?

3. Experience For Avoidance: Was this decision a result of my lack of experience? Or did it come about because I decided not to decide? Why did I want to avoid making it? How can I learn to be more proactive and less of a procrastinator?

4. Help Wanted: Did I have all the information I needed to make this decision? Are there people who could have given me expert input? If I establish a policy of factoring in cushion time between the opportunity and the decision, would that result in a better product, outcome or conclusion?

Why Review?

At the beginning of this book we imagined being seated on a commercial airplane, traveling swiftly to an unknown destination. Suppose you were flying somewhere and the pilot took you where you didn't want to go? Would you fly that airline again? You probably wouldn't feel like you were in friendly skies.

Similarly, to become better at making your best decision, you must look at your travel habits. Have you been getting where you want to go on a regular basis?

Reviewing practices and options keeps your skills sharp and reminds you that you are the pilot. Yes, time flies but you are the navigator. A vice president of a major corporation recently was quoted as saying,

"I don't know how much faster and harder we all can go. There has to be a breaking point."

That same individual started reviewing her course one day when she was in an airport rushing between flights. Suddenly she darted into a book store and picked up an inspirational book as if she could choke down inwardness and peace in a nanosecond. Instead her eyes started stinging with tears as she realized, much like the person on a plane going where the pilot wants to go, she didn't have control. [2]

All You Need To Know

Occasionally reviewing circumstances, purpose, mission, vision, and choices will give you strategies to help you reach your desired destination. Julie Bick wrote a book called *All I Really Need To Know In Business I Learned At Microsoft.* At 33 Bick was one of the Microsofties who was helping to revolutionize the computer industry. Her husband, Rogers Weed, also worked at Microsoft.

At the height of enviable lucrative careers they both did something reporter Katharine Mieszkowski calls radical. They took a "Radical Sabbatical" for one year. During a 10 week trek through Asia, Julie conceived the idea for her now successful book which eventually launched a writing and speaking career. Her husband later returned to Microsoft. "It's easy to put your head down, look up 20 years later, and wonder about all the things you didn't do." Rogers said. "The time off helped me gain perspective." [3]

To review is to gain perspective again and again. It is a step we must never outgrow or leave behind if we wish to become confident and sure in our decisions. Julie Bick's book is refreshing and insightful. In a chapter called "Keep it in Perspective" she tells of a former boss who would march down the halls at 10 PM when employees were working late. "Is this our youth? Is this how we want to spend out youth?" she would yell and then encourage them to go home! [4]

Sometimes Review is Preview

I have a friend who is always in a rush. One day she dashed to the garage, jumped in her car and pressed the button that operates the electric door. She was busy fastening her seat belt and jamming the gear shift quickly into position while mentally going over her notes for a morning board meeting.

She proceeded to step on the gas without a glance at the mirror, which would have revealed that the door only opened one-fourth of the way. Imagine the impact as she proceeded to slam into that steel door.

Sometimes you have to look back to go forward. If my friend had glanced for a nanosecond into her review mirror, she could have made a wise decision: Don't go!

Reviewing our decisions is like looking in a rear view mirror for safety purposes.

Reviewing the Steps:

Review the Decision making steps that we have covered in this book.

1. Focus

2. Explore

3. Choose

4. Act

5. Evaluate

6. Review

Deciders and Delayers

Congratulations if you are feeling more confident and more decisive. Decisive people make more money, have more fun, find more time, experience less stress, get more done, love their jobs, meet every deadline, have no regrets and live in balance.

On the other hand, indecisive people are delayers. Delayers tend to overspend, lose their joy, run out of time, feel anxious, never catch up, complain about their jobs, have trouble being on time, constantly second-guess themselves, and long for more balance in life.

Decisive People

Make More Money: Bill Gates, Warren Buffett and Paul Allen have something in common. First of all they have more money than other Americans. In the order listed, they are the wealthiest people in the United States, monetarily speaking. They have something else in common, they are decisive. Read biographical information about them and you will learn they habitually surround themselves with people who are also confident deciders.

Other decisive people I have interviewed may not have $21 billion dollars like Buffet or $17 billion like Allen, but they have all the money they want. There is a Proverb that says, "Lord, Give me neither extreme poverty nor excessive riches. Otherwise, I may have too much and disown you or I may become poor and steal and dishonor the name of my God." [5]

Decisive people don't have money just for the sake of having money. They use it to change and better the lives of others and the condition of the world. One corporate king gives his employees large bonuses and ownership in the company. Another gives huge amounts to a variety of charitable organizations.

Still other decisive people attract wealth but give it all to the work they love. When Mother Teresa was given an expensive car, she used it for her work.

Marsha Sinetar, Ph.D., an organizational psychologist says, *Do What You Love, The Money Will Follow,* and that is the title of a book she wrote. She's right. Decisive people do what they love. They spend themselves and use their unique talent in service to others and they are magnets for the kind of wealth that is important to them. They don't allow money to become a burden. They are not defined by wealth.

Have More Fun: Decisive people enjoy what they do and do what they enjoy. They are not waiting for things to be perfect before they are content. Delayers say, "When I get a better job, I'll be happy. When I lose a few pounds, I'll go out and live it up. When I don't have to care for aging parents or sick kids, then I'll radiate joy. Someday. Someday."

Decisive people know someday is now. They don't take themselves too seriously. Just seriously enough.

Find More Time: Look at the life of a confident decision maker. Usually they are not the ones who say, "I'm overwhelmed!" or "I'm just too busy to talk to you!"

I have spoken with celebrities, authors, CEO's, teachers and those from all walks of life who have time consuming responsibilities. Successful entrepreneurs, millionaires, religious leaders, whatever the profession, decisive people always find time to do what matters most.

They have eliminated the URGENT! and IMPERATIVE! and live the IMPORTANT and INTERESTING. When I contacted Howard Putnam or Harvey MacKay or Jeff Davidson I expected them to say, "I am too busy to talk to you!"

But just the opposite happened. Many times busy people answer their own phone.

I read that Conrad Hilton used to take the time to pick up litter in front of his hotels if he was in town. And he would stop and talk to the employees, encouraging them and giving them tips on success.

Sam Walton would take the time to mingle with associates at Wal-Mart stores all over the United States. Decisive people have exactly the same amount of time that indecisive people have. Twenty-four hours every day. They TAKE time instead of letting time rule them.

Experience Less Stress: According to the American Academy of Family Physicians, stress may be "the greatest single contributor to illness in the late 20th century."

One in seven people are hospitalized each year for stress related disorders. Two-thirds of office visits to doctors are related to unrelieved stress and its effects on the mind and body. Stress makes life a joyless struggle and can result in a whole range of physical and mental disease.

Some examples are tension headaches, heartburn and anxiety attacks, ulcers, heart disease and severe depression. Stress can even result in sudden death caused by the heart stopping.

One of the greatest causes of stress is the inability to make a decision. Decisions create closure. Closure comforts. Comfort relieves stress. Decisive people experience closure, completion and the resulting comfort because their confident choices free them to let go of the past and move on to more exciting choices!

They do away with stress by:

1. Taking control.

2. Setting realistic goals.

3. Sticking to priorities

4. Not overbooking the calendar

5. Exchanging the words "I Must" and "I Should" for "I CHOOSE TO!"

6. Laughing more

7. Doing what they love.

Get More Done: Decisive people know if they don't choose to use they choose to lose. They carefully pick out events worthy of time and effort because if they don't decide how to use their moments, someone or something else will.

They know there is a difference between interruptions and distractions. Interruptions are opportunities, are brief and complement projects. Distractions drag on, are unrelated and end in frustration.

Decisive people don't waste time patting

themselves on the back or reading their own clippings. They look at themselves with sober judgement, keep a light touch, turn the page and move on. Satisfaction breeds accomplishment.

Love Their Jobs: "Choosing our work allows us to enter into that work willingly, enthusiastically, and mindfully. Whatever our work is, whether we love it or not, we can choose to do it well, to be with it – moment to moment – to combat the temptation to back away from being fully present. As we practice this art and attitude, we also grow more capable of enjoying work itself!"[6]

Meet Every Deadline: Decisive people meet every deadline because they are in charge. If the deadline is not realistic, they can change it!

One bumper sticker says IF YOU ARE NOT WINNING THE GAME, CHANGE THE RULES! Best selling author, James Dobson, once reordered priorities when working on a manuscript. Family responsibilities caused him to make arrangements with editors to change the deadline. His book came out a year later than expected. It was a great hit, the timing was perfect, the publishing house was pleased and Dobson still knows he made the best decision when he pushed back a deadline.

Knowing who is in charge causes decisive people to be less stressed about outward pressures.

Therefore, they rarely change the rules! Because confident decision making breeds confidence, deciders trust their own intuition, experience, and ability to find resources that support their priorities. They are free to create and complete and manage multiple and competing time demands.

Have No Regrets! Everything works together for good when done with integrity and a desire to live within one's life purpose and calling. There is no such thing as a regrettable decision. No need to second guess. Every accomplishment is a learning opportunity. The scientist who repeats his experiment 100 times without expected results now knows 100 variations and when 101 is the perfect result, he does not regret the first 100 attempts. They were not wrong decisions. They were stepping stones on the ladder of learning.

Decisive people know that every decision is a building block and every effort to make better decisions is mortar in the construction project of life.

Decisive people are so full they have no room for regret!

Live In Balance: Margins and breathing space and pacing mean something to secure deciders. They say, "YES!" more often than delayers. They also say, "No!" just about as often. Balance comes naturally when a person knows what is important and what is insignificant.

Remember being on a teeter-totter as a child and your friend decided all of a sudden to go home for lunch when you were up in the air? Whooooooooosch! You hit the ground hard and it was not fun. Decisive people give and take. They weigh opportunities and options.

They are not grounded or weighed down or let down often. But when they are, they know there is another opportunity and option around the corner. Decisive people know their own limitations. They do their best and give what they have to their priorities and life purpose.

Living in harmony. Equalizing debits and credits. Understanding the ebb and flow. Always learning, absorbing and then pouring forth. Deciders know how to balance competing demands so they never give up anything that is important or ignore something that deserves attention.

Summary

❑ Reviewing is previewing.

❑ Look back to move forward. Use that rear view mirror.

❑ Learn from the past but build to the future.

❑ Be a dedicated decider, not a distracted delayer.

SEVEN

D.E.C.I.D.E.!

It's much better to make too many decisions than not enough decisions. Whatever you do, don't be like the person who said, "I used to be indecisive, but now I'm not so sure." [1]

D. E. C. I. D. E. !

Here is another way of remembering the six steps: Focus, Explore, Choose, Act, Evaluate, Review. If you have not memorized those six steps you need to. Perhaps this acronym will stay in your mind because it spells

DECIDE!

D etermine your challenge.
E xamine your options.
C onstruct a plan.
I mplement it!
D iscern the value.
E stimate results.

DETERMINE your challenge: Remember the importance of FOCUS. Narrow your focus to concentrate energy and vision on the task at hand. Make sure you can focus and zero in on your destination so you won't run the risk of reaching the wrong destination. Always ask yourself "why?" until you have a crystal clear focus. Make sure your challenges line up with your purpose, mission and vision for life.

EXAMINE your options: Search for ideas. Explore selections and variations. Gather information and resources. Talk to people. Visit places. Research papers. Give yourself a realistic time limit to gather information and options. You will never have all the statistics or knowledge available on the planet, so know when to stop. Consider all options. Remind yourself often that you are endowed with a great and powerful gift. The power to choose. You do have choices, options, selections. Consider them.

CONSTRUCT a plan: Now it is time to CHOOSE one of the options and construct a plan. Don't look back or second guess at this point. Choose only one option. Create the future with your confident decisions. You are in charge. You can turn left or right. My husband used to say, "There are only two ways to go when you are driving down the highway in your car. The right way and the wrong way. If you are going the wrong way, turn around and go the right way! Life is like that!"

IMPLEMENT your plan! Don't allow your decision to atrophy. ACT on your choice. You have focused on a challenge, you have explored your options, you have chosen and constructed one scheme. Do it. Allowing too much time between choice and action will water down or delete decisions. Move ahead. Clear the way for more and better decisions as you learn and build.

DISCERN the value of your decision. Was it a winner? Can you improve on it next time? List the positive effects and how you felt after completion. Evaluate the procedure and the profit. Write down benefits. Make notes, if necessary, for future related projects. Now is not the time to second-guess. Evaluation is not second-guessing. It is positive examination. It can also be a much needed pat on your back. You are becoming more confident.

ESTIMATE results. Look back to move forward. Learn from the past to build for the future. To review is to see again with new eyes. We have come full circle. To review and estimate results is to revisit step number one. Focus. You want to continually focus on your purpose. You want to attend to your mission. You want to live your vision – your dream with details. Remember that purpose is destination, mission is map, and vision is vehicle. Where am I going? What road should I take when there are so many roads? How will I get there safely and successfully? Focus, Explore, Choose, Act, Evaluate, Review. Determine, Examine, Construct, Implement, Discern, Estimate.

BE DECISIVE!

Where you stand and where you land in the future is being determined now. Whether you succeed or fail in your own eyes or through the lens of history may well depend on decisions you make today. Only you can choose what sort of person you want to become. You are the one who can determine how much risk you are willing to undertake.

Be brave. Don't leave your tomorrows to chance, circumstance, companions, crowds or any influence outside yourself and your Creator. You have been gifted with the power of choice. Cherish the gift. Life is not what happens to you. Life is a work of art you create from ingredients of circumstance. Make life exciting and productive. Make your life count for eternity. Mold your moments to the shape of your dreams. How?

Be Decisive!

Lou Ann Smith
Cameron Park, California
January, 1999

Footnotes

Chapter One: Focus

1.   Charles Bradshaw and Dave Gilbert, *Too Hurried To Love*, HARVEST HOUSE PUBLISHERS, 1991 pp.36-37

2.   Photorefractive Keratectomy Surgery for Nearsightedness with Astigmatism (PRKa). For information phone Pacific Laser Eye Center (916) 635-4878

3.   Roy Saunderson, *How To Focus On Success!*, RECOGNITION MANAGEMENT INSTITUTE, Canada pp.55; 71-75

4.   Henry David Thoreau, *Walden and Other Writings* (New York: Bantam Books, 1962), p.132 quoted by Jean Flemming in *Between Walden and the Whirlwind:The key to order in an overwhelming world.* Navpress 1987, p.44

Chapter Two: Explore

1.   Calvin Miller, *The Empowered Leader* (BROADMAN & HOLMAN PUBLISHERS, Nashville, Tenessee 1995) p.76

2.   Patricia Sellers, *The 50 Most Powerful Women In American Business*, (FORTUNE Magazine, 10/12/98)p.76

3.   Howard Putnam, *The Winds of Turbulence* (HARPER BUSINESS, 1991) pp 170-171

4.   Joe Griffith, *Speaker's Library of Business*, (PRENTICE HALL, NJ, 1990) p.115

5.   Herbert Prochnow, *Treasury of Inspiration* (BAKER BOOKHOUSE, Michigan) p.215

6.   Author Unknown, *Eleanor Doan Speaker's Sourcebook* (ZONDERVAN, 1960) p.139

7.   John Dalla Costa, *The Ethical Imperative* (ADDISON WESLEY, 1998) p.21

8.   As reported by Frank Bucaro, Professional Speaker, 1998 in a keynote address.

Chapter Three: Choose

1. Richard Ford, *Saying goodbye to the moment*, The Sacramento Bee Sunday edition, January 3, 1999, Forum 3

2. A paraphrase of Richard Foster's quote: "The disciplined person is the person who can do what needs to be done when it needs to be done. The disciplined person is the person who can live in the appropriateness of the hour...The disciplined person is the free person." –from *Reasons to Be Glad* as quoted in *Discipleship Journal*.

3. Virginia Brasier, in *Eleanor Doan's Speakers Source Book* p.266

4. This question was put to Zadig by the Grand Magi in *Zadig, A Mystery of Fate*.

5. Donna Britt, *There's no turning back on life's road*, The Sacramento Bee, January 20, 1999, E2

6. Annie Dillard as quoted by Jean Flemming, *Between Walden and the Whirlwind* p.43

7. Reported in *Discipleship Journal*, Issue sixty-five, 1991

8. Calvin Miller, *The Empowered Leader*, p.71

9. Stephanie Culp, *Streamlining Your Life*, p.49

10. Stephen R. Covey, *First Things First*, (SIMON & SCHUSTER, 1995) p. 321

11. Philemon 7, (for complete text see *New International Version of the Holy Bible*, (ZONDERVAN, 1978) p. 1109

12. Calvin Miller, ibid.

13. John 15: 13-15

Author's note: Onesimus means "useful."

Chapter Four: Act

1. Nathan Myhrvold quoted by Anna Muoio in *FAST COMPANY*, June:July 1998 issue 15, p.84

2. Quinnn Spitzer & Ron Evans, *Heads You Win: How the Best Companies Think* (SIMON & SCHUSTER, 1997) p. 75

3. Source Unknown

4. Stephanie Culp, *Streamlining Your Life: A 5-point plan for uncomplicated living*, (WRITER'S DIGEST BOOKS, 1991) p. 35

5.   Stedman Graham, *You Can Make It Happen*, (FIRESIDE; SIMON & SCHUSTER, 1997), p. 224

6.   Lou Ann Smith, *Building Miracles*, (NAB Today Magazine, January/February 1999) cover story, p.1

Chapter Five: Evaluate

1.   Quoted from cover synopsis, *It's A Wonderful Life*, The Congress Video Group, 1986

2.   *Heads You Win*, p.60

3.   Jeff Davidson, *Breathing Space,: Living and Working at a Comfortable pace in a Sped-Up Society* (MASTER MEDIA BOOKS 1991).

4.   Charles E. Hummel, *Tyranny of the Urgent* (InterVarsity Press, Illinois 1967)

5.   Laura Berman Fortgang, *Take Yourself to the Top*, (WARNER BOOKS, 1998) p.206

Chapter Six: Review

1.   Roger von Oech, *A Whack on the Side of the Head*, (WARNER BOOKS, 1983,19900) p. 74

2.   Melinda Brown, quoted in *Balancing Acts*, (FAST COMPANY, February:March 1999) p. 86

3.   Katherine Mieszkowski, *Radical Sabbaticals*, (Ibid. November:December 1998) p.48

4.   Julie Bick, *All I Really Need To Know In Business I Learned At Microsoft*, (POCKET BOOKS BUSINESS, 1997) p.157

5.   Proverbs 30: 8 & 9

6.   Marsha Sinetar, *Do What You Love, The Money Will Follow*, (DELL PUBLISHING, BANTAM DOUBLEDAY, New York, 1987) p.13

Chapter Seven: D. E .C. I. D. E.

1.   Larry Winget, *The Simple Way To Success*, (Win Publications, Tulsa Oklahoma 1996) p.13

Words Of Wisdom
(Quotes And Quips From Wise Guys)*

•   Many of the answers to your dreams are inside of you. –Roy Saunderson, *How To Focus On Success* p.82

•   The key to making your goals real is to dream big, keep it simple, start small and work on it every day. Ibid. p.85

•   It's much better to make too many decisions than not enough decisions. Whatever you do, don't be like the person who said, "I used to be indecisive, but now I'm not so sure." Larry Winget, *The Simple Way To Success* p.13

•   Your decisions, right or wrong, create places for you to start again. Calvin Miller, *The Empowered Leader* p.79

•   One of the best ways decisions serve is to provide a strong sense of self. They do this by summoning, from your innermost being, the ego force necessary to make these awesome decisions. Ibid.

•   Keeping God close at hand will avoid a circuitous, indecisive life. Ibid.

About The Author

L OU ANN SMITH is a freelance writer and motivational speaker. Internationally known as a powerful communicator, Lou Ann Smith uses humor and clarity to address topics such as **Change, Communication and Customer Service**. She is a professional member of the National Speakers Association and can be reached on line at louannsmit@aol.com or through the NSA website: www.nsaspeaker.org or for more information on Lou Ann Smith's speaking services contact:

Joyfully Speaking"
3306 Flame Ct.
Cameron Park, CA 95682
530 677-1398
louannsmit@aol.com

Acknowledgments

Thank you...

Dr. Richard Cantor for being my wonderful eye doctor, a great decision maker, and for enabling me to BE DECISIVE! and have PRKa Laser surgery which changed my life and brought new focus to everything I do!

Norman Rohrer for being my first real writing mentor and encouraging me to write long works (like a book) and short ones (like a two word epitaph).

Kirby for sharing 26 years of the best decision ever: us. For your patience and support while I write, speak, travel and whine. Thank you.

Jim and Barbara Weems for your creativity and enthusiasm about this project. Jacqueline Savell for your editing skills and Stephen Savell and Dustin Smith for all the ongoing encouragement.

Jeff Davidson, I never met you in person but our telephone and E-mail conversations were such a help! You are a National Speakers Association colleague and because I read your book years ago, I have enough "Breathing Space" to live my dreams and write them down.

Finally, to the Lord of John 3:16 who inspires every thought: Praise and thanks.

End Note: The greatest effort has been made to give credit for every quote and concept used within these pages. Anecdotes have been edited and some names changed for privacy reasons. My thanks to those who shared decision-making stories to make this book a help and guide for readers.

Please feel free to contact me:

E-Mail: louannsmit@aol.com

Snail Mail: Lou Ann Smith
c/o **Change Your Life Books**
P.O. Box: General Delivery
Rescue, California 95672

☑ **Yes** I want to share this book with others!

SEND THIS FORM ALONG WITH PAYMENT TO
LOU ANN SMITH

CYL BOOKS | **Change Your Life Books**
P. O. Box 287
Rescue, CA 95672

Order today and **SAVE**
**Pay $15.95 now and Lou Ann will
ship it to you FREE**

		Qty	Each	Amount
BE DECISIVE! *A Six Step Formula*			$15.95	
For Making Your Best Decisions Every Time!			Sub Total	
Quantity discounts			S/H	00
are available on bulk purchases			**TOTAL**	

Name _____ Date _____

Company _____ E-mail _____

Street Address _____

City/Province _____ State _____

Zip/Postal Code _____ Country _____ Phone _____

☐ **VISA** ☐ **MasterCard** ☐ Check/Money Order (*Payable to CYL Books*)

Card No. / / / / / / / / / / / / / / / / / /

Exp. date _____ Signature _____